KURT E. KOCH D.D.

BETWEEN CHRIST AND SATAN

1 9 6 1
All rights reserved
Printed by H. Wolf, Oehringen/Wbg.
Germany

# BETWEEN CHRIST
# AND SATAN

by

KURT E. KOCH D.D.

EVANGELIZATION PUBLISHERS

Berghausen Bd. (Germany)

# Contents

|  |  | Page |
|---|---|---|
| 1. | Preface of the Translator | 9 |
| 2. | Preface of the Author | 11 |

## A. FORTUNE-TELLING . . . 13

| I. | Astrology | 13 |
| II. | Cartomancy | 23 |
| III. | Palmistry | 32 |
| IV. | Divining Rod and Pendulum | 39 |
| V. | Mirror Mantic | 53 |
| VI. | Psychometry | 57 |
| VII. | The Position of the Bible | 60 |
| VIII. | The Deliverance | 62 |

## B. MAGIC

| I. | Concept of Magic | 71 |
|  | 1. Dispute about the Existence of Magic | 72 |
|  | 2. Extrasensory Ways of Magic | 73 |
|  | 3. Objects of Magic | 74 |
| II. | Origin, Aim and Development of Magic | 77 |
|  | 1. The Arch-Temptation | 77 |
|  | 2. Origin of Magic Powers | 78 |

III. Forms of Magic . . . . . . . . . . 82
    1. Criminal Hypnosis . . . . . . 82
    2. Mental Suggestion . . . . . . . 85
    3. Magically-based Mesmerism . . . 87
    4. Main Forms of Magic . . . . . . 84

IV. Areas of Applied Magic . . . . . . 98
    1. Healing and Bringing on Sickness . 98
    2. Love and Hate Magic . . . . . . 101
    3. Persecution and Defence Magic . . 102
    4. Casting and Breaking Spells . . . 103
    5. Death Magic on Animals and Humans 105

V. The Magic Rites . . . . . . . . 107
    1. Magic Liturgy . . . . . . . . 107
    2. Magic Symbolism . . . . . . . 108
    3. The Magic Word . . . . . . . 110
    4. The Magic Ritual . . . . . . . 112

VI. Effects of Magic and How to Overcome
    Them . . . . . . . . . . . . . 112
    1. The Principle of Compensation . . 113
    2. The Wrong Defence . . . . . . 114
    3. The Spiritual Weapons . . . . . 115
    4. The Deliverance through Christ . . 117


C. SPIRITISM . . . . . . . 123

I. Psychic Phenomena . . . . . . . 125
    1. Spiritistic Visions . . . . . . . 126
    2. Table-Lifting . . . . . . . . 127

3. Glass-Moving . . . . . . . . 129
4. Automatic Writing . . . . . 130
5. Speaking in Trance . . . . . 131
6. Materialization . . . . . . . 132
7. Excursion of the Psyche . . . . . 134

II. Physical Phenomena . . . . . . 136
8. Telekinesis . . . . . . . . 137
9. Levitation . . . . . . . 137
10. Apports . . . . . . . . . 138

III. Spiritistic-Magic Phenomena . . . . 140
11. Magic Persecution . . . . . 141
12. Magic Defence . . . . . . . 143

IV. Metaphysical Phenomena . . . . . 144
13. Apparitions . . . . . . . 144
14. Objective, Locality-Bound Spook . 147

V. Cultic Phenomena . . . . . . . 149
15. Spiritistic Cult . . . . . . 149
16. Spiritism among Christians . . . 150

VI. Judging Spiritistic Phenomena . . . 153
1. From the View of Medicine and
Psychology . . . . . . . 153
2. From the View of the Bible . . 153
3. From the View of Christian
Counseling . . . . . . . . 156
4. The Setting Free Through Christ . . 159

D. OCCULT LITERATURE . . 167

E.  DIVINE HEALING TODAY    183

1. Biblical Meaning of James 5 . . .    183
2. Magic and Suggestive Healings . .    186
3. Biblical Healing Miracles . . . .    196


F.  REPORTS OF BIBLICAL
    HEALINGS and
    DELIVERANCES . . . . .    200

 1. Christ, the Victor over Dark Powers    200
 2. The Bulwarks of Darkness . . . .    203
 3. The Works of the Devil . . . . .    207
 4. Incurably Insane . . . . . . .    211
 5. Remember Not the Sins of My Youth    214
 6. Jesus Redeems . . . . . . . .    217
 7. Delivered from the Power of Darkness    222
 8. Battle with a Possessed Woman . .    226
 9. The Stronger One . . . . . . .    235
10. If the Son therefore Shall Make
    You Free . . . . . . . . . .    238
11. In My Name Shall They Cast Out
    Devils . . . . . . . . . . .    241
12. The Victory of Christ . . . . . .    245
13. There is Power in the Blood . . .    246
14. Deprived of Power ... . . . . .    249
15. The Name of Jesus ... . . . . .    252

## Preface of the translator

Dr. Kurt E. Koch is a German minister and evangelist. Through his extensive counseling activities he came into particular contact with the field of psychic subjection. For thirty years he made the observation that occupation with occult things (fortune-telling, necromancy, spiritism) is not only a harmless pastime but often leads to serious psychic and nervous disturbances.

His observations were published in a scientific work "Seelsorge und Okkultismus" (Christian Counseling and Occultism). Within a short time the book went through six editions and became a theological best-seller. It is valued as an authority in its field. This book was also the occasion of hundreds of invitations which Dr. Koch received, leading him into all European countries except Russia. Dr. Koch lectured at 26 European universities before theologians and medical men, psychologists and scientists. His lectures often started stormy discussions. Beyond all consent and rejection the fruit of his work has been the fact, that his questionings can no longer be hushed up.

Beside this lecturing activity he wrote 27 books and pamphlets, all of which have reached high editions. A few of his more popular writings are assembled in this book. The problems portrayed here are not only a typical European growth, but have their parallels also in the United States and in the whole world.

Yolanda N. Entz

## Preface of the author

The well-known English writer C.S. Lewis writes in his preface to his book "The Screwtape Letters":

"There are two equal and opposite errors into which our race can fall about the devils. One is to disbelieve in their existence. The other is to believe, and to feel an excessive and unhealthy interest in them."

The ones are the rationalists of every shading, the others are the magicians. Both will get upset about this book. Do they have reasons to be upset? Reason to be shocked has the Christian counselor who in his counseling sessions sees the devastating fruit of materialism and magic. Therefore this information must be made public. There are two motives for this.

We have to proclaim the victory of Jesus Christ over all the powers of darkness. Oppressed and occultly subjected people cannot be helped through medicine, psychology and psychiatry but only through Jesus Christ. Therefore they have to be shown the way to the Great Deliverer.

Permission was granted for the publication of examples from Christian counseling.

The Author

# A. FORTUNE-TELLING

For thousands of years fortune-telling has been a bastard of heathenism, born of fear, curiosity and superstition. Fortune-telling in our time is a manifold problem of folklore, psychology and theology. The starting-point of these expositions is the Christian counseling work of the Protestant theologian. The Protestant ministry offers always new experience material. My file of occult cases has grown already to over 3000 cases. Scientific dissertations are being avoided in this book. They can be found in my book "Seelsorge und Okkultismus" (Christian Counseling and Occultism). Mainly first-hand examples are given here to help the reader form his own opinion. The seal of confession is not being violated, for permission for anonymous publishing has been received. The following areas of fortune-telling will be discussed: Astrology, cartomancy, palmistry, divining rods and pendulums, mirror mantic, psychometry, the position of the Bible, liberation from occult subjection.

## I. ASTROLOGY

E 1.   A woman appeared at a police station and stated that she had shot her son to death. An astrologer had declared in a written horoscope that her ill son would never regain his full mental strength.

Because she had wanted to save her son from this terrible future, she had killed him. The woman was arrested and sentenced after a long trial. The astrologer himself went free.

This every-day experience shows the suggestive powers and the effects of horoscope casting. Before we get into this problematic field, first a brief historical introduction.

One understands under astrology the prophecy of human character and fate from the constellation of the stars. It is the most widely-spread superstition of our time. The Research Institute of Public Opinion at Bodensee established through a questionnaire that about 63% of the German people had already occupied themselves with astrology. Very few of them know about the so-called scientific form of astrology, most of them subscribe to the rank solstitial point horoscope.

In the ancient world astronomy, the exploration of the stars and astrology, the interpretation of the constellation of the stars, was a single science. In the ancient Babylonic Empire it was the science of the priests. Originally horoscopes were cast only for kings. Since astrology could also be traced into the areas of old Mexican culture, it is thought that one meets here with a common human aspect (archtype). The Greeks and Romans took over astrology from the Babylonians. Of course at that time there were already rational thinkers who ridiculed astrology. The poet Ennius declares: "Horoscopes cost one drachme and are one drachme too expensive." The church father Augustin called astrology the craziest delusion of mankind.

During the Middle Ages Europe was seized by astrology. The Staufen Emperor Frederick II, was especially controlled by it. Professorial chairs for astrology were established. Even the reformer Philip Melanchthon occupied one. But Luther called it "a shabby art." Out of that age we are told the story of how the astrologer Stoeffler was stultified hopelessly for all time. He predicted a diluvian flood for February 1524. The population was terrified. Nobody wanted to work. The fields were not tilled. The rich had ships built for themselves or moved up into the high mountains. The Great Elector Frederick William of Brandenburg also made preparations for his escape.

Even the great astronomer Kepler was not free from astrology. One of his well-known examples is the prediction that Wallenstein would die a peaceful death in his 70th year. But he was killed in his 50th year. But Kepler engaged in astrology only because of economic necessity. He wrote: "Astrology is to me an unbearable but necessary slavery. To keep my yearly income, my title and my living quarters, I have to comply with ignorant curiosity. Astronomy is the wise mother and astrology the foolish daughter who gives herself to everyone that pays her, so that she can support her wise mother."

Since the age of rationalism (1750) the astrological movement receded. Astronomy and astrology came to a final parting. The two World Wars made it flare up again. In 1930 already horoscopes were cast for Hitler, which were very contradictory. After 1933 his influence should have been declining. The "truth" of these horoscopes we have certainly experienced. That astrologer miscalculated by twelve years, but they were disastrous twelve years. The horoscope of Rudolf Hess prophecied that he was destined by fate to bring about a reconciliation with England. That was perhaps the reason why he flew to England. The truth of this horoscope is equally well known as Hitler's.

How does astrology look today? One distinguishes between a supposedly scientific form, which for instance Alfred Rosenberg (Signs in the Sky) advocates, and a popular form, the so-called solstitial point horoscope. This mentally contagious habit is so widely spread, that the big daily newspapers and magazines have to take it into account. We are told that in the United States some 170 newspapers and magazines carry daily horoscopes. It is also known that there are about 25 000 well-paid astrologers.

A humorous example shall give us an insight into the situation.

E 2   It happened at a big conference of Protestant ministers, where I participated. Publishers of big newspapers and many journalists were invited. The discussion was about the intellectual level and outlook on life of the newspapers. A minister pointed out that the Swedish newspaper men do not bring any horoscopes in their papers. In all of Sweden they had accepted this decision. Why could not that be possible in Germany and in other countries? The chief editor of a large daily paper stood up and gave the following explanation. Personally he was convinced of the nonsense of astrology but it was a financial question. The paper which does not bring the weekly horoscope in its Sunday edition must count on many cancellations. No newspaper could afford this. Then he told laughingly of a funny experience. One Friday the astrologer's horoscope did not arrive in time. In this dilemma he went to a storage room and picked out an old horoscope. Since he did not know the Zodiac in order, it was a wrong one. In spite of this none of the readers noticed the mistake. Since all went well, he saved himself the astrologer's fee and for 22 times he used wrong horoscopes from the past years. None of the hundred thousand readers found it out, till finally someone wrote in that it could not be right that the sign of Scorpion rules in July. Now his wiles were uncovered. Again he had to get the help of the "experts". This was the report of the editor. Then he added laughingly: "During the time of the wrong horoscopes, it still was all right. It does not depend on the horoscope but on what man believes."

2. What reasons do we have as Christians not to recognize astrology as being providential to our

fate? First of all we are repelled by the heathenistic background. With the ancient people astrology had a religious accent. The stars were equivalent with gods. The heathen knew himself to be led, influenced or threatened by these planet gods. In the course of the ages the religious character of astrology receded but the old rules were kept.

Thus we have already the second reason. The keeping of the old rules includes an insoluble contradiction. In 26000 years the axis of the earth prescribes the lateral area of a cone (precession). Today's astrologer does not see the planets at the same place as his colleague of 4000 to 5000 years ago. Beside this several other planets were discovered, Uranus in 1781, Neptune in 1839, and Pluto in 1932. Since all these changes failed to shake the astrological system in any way, present astronomers reject astrology as one of the greatest frauds of all time.

With this the line of astrological impossibilities has not at all been completed. The rays of the stars meeting the child in the moment of birth shall be decisive of his fate. In this assertion are several fantastic notions. Our earth is being reached predominantly by light and cosmic rays. But both of these types of rays do not come from the planets which have no light of their own. The light comes from the sources of light, which are the fixed stars. Cosmic rays come from the Milky Way. Our planets as our earth do not radiate.

Moreover, the moment the umbilical cord is cut

should be of decisive importance. Therefore when the doctor delays the cutting of the cord, then that human being receives a different fate. One should then let the astrologer calculate the time when the doctor should cut the cord of the newborn, so that the child may have the most favourable fate. The next question is, why the 250 people whose cords are cut at the same moment, do not have the same fate. There was only one Goethe, one Johann Sebastian Bach among the many that were born at the same time. A well-known astrology researcher, Abbe Moritz Warburg, declared ironically: Astrologers can certainly never be discredited.

A reform movement of astrology wants to clear the way of these difficulties. It is called Cosmo-Biology, with headquarters in Aalen, Wuerttemberg. Man's heredity must be equally considered as the constellation of the planets. This is a compromise suggestion of the old astrology.

Of course there is no question that there are certain interplanetary connections between other planets and our earth. The tides and other natural phenomena have their cause in them. To look for these connections to be influential to our life and fate, would have the same significance as if we would assert that our wrist watch with its radium dial would cause our radio-active death.

3. The main problems of astrology are in the area of Christian counseling. It can be stated in three

words: Swindle - suggestion - demonry. To each word an example from my counseling practice.

E 3  A student of psychology at the Sorbonne University in Paris wanted to write his thesis. He put a classified advertisement in a big newspaper and passed himself off as an astrologer. For a pre-paid fee of 2000 francs ($ 5) he would cast a detailed horoscope for each writer. He received about 400 letters, and with that the financing of his studies was secured. He cast a single horoscope for all 400 customers, without paying any attention to the signs of the Zodiac. He only considered psychological aspects: to tell everybody about a good future, then they won't be sorry for the fee; to admit positive character traits to everybody, for everybody likes to believe that, etc. This horoscope he sent to all of his 400 customers. He received many letters of appreciation, since he had covered almost everybody's situation. Then the student wrote his dissertation and got his degree with honors. — In this case astrology was a crafty business. The young Frenchman earned much money and a doctor title through the stupidity and superstition of his fellowmen.

E 4  The craziest example of the horoscope disease I met in the person of a young theologian. As a young man this minister was a merchant. He had a detailed horoscope cast, in which it was said, that he would change his job three times. The young merchant did not have to be told twice. He attended evening schools and then studied Protestant theology and was ordained as a minister. He married and fortunately did not have any children. Why that was fortunate must be told quickly. After a few years he was converted to the Catholic faith and was taken over as a Catholic priest. His wife was allowed to stay with him as his housekeeper. Already two changes of jobs are behind him. He explains that he has not reached his last station as yet. He feels an urge to get into a fourth profession. His plans are not complete yet. It will not be very long before the change will have taken place. — In this case this unfortunate man became a victim of a suggestion. He lives out his horoscope. He stands under the compulsion and ban of this astrological prediction.

E 5    A minister who sees his mission in fighting superstition had a horoscope cast for the sake of study. He wanted to prove that horoscope casting is swindle and superstition. He paid a big fee because a detailed horoscope had been cast for him. Now he waited confidently that the horoscope would not fulfil itself, for that was his opinion. But he was amazed to see that the prophecies fulfilled themselves. For eight years he could observe that all predictions came true, even to the smallest details. He grew uneasy at this and reflected about this puzzle. It had indeed been his preconceived opinion that everything was based on suggestion and superstition. Impossible that he as a Christian could be a victim of this suggestion. Finally he knew no other way of escape than to repent and ask God for His protection. The thought came to him, that he had sinned through this experiment and had placed himself under the influence of dark powers. After his repentance he discovered to his surprize that now his horoscope was no longer correct. — Through this experience the minister understood clearly that demonic powers are active in astrology. The person who exposes himself to danger will perish in it.

4. How do experts in different fields judge astrology? Medicine already recognizes the damages done by astrology. The medical superintendent Dr. Schrank of Wiesbaden writes in an article about the psychology of superstition: "How dangerous the effects of astrology are, is proved by the fact, that in sensitive people serious psychic disturbances, fear of life, despair and disorders have been observed. Astrology paralyzes initiative and power of judgment. It stupefies and encourages shallowness. It uniforms the personality for a platitudenous underground movement."

Astrologers themselves have said it even more clearly. The leading astrologer Wehrle designates astrology as mantic, i. e. fortune-telling art. Thus in astrology we are faced with an occult tendency with all the effects that occult things carry along with them.

The Bible makes it most clear what is to be thought of astrology. In Deuteronomy 17, 2—5 it is commanded: "Who worships either the sun or moon, or any of the host of heaven, shall be stoned." The prophet Isaiah speaks even more in detail about astrology. He writes in Isaiah 47, 13—14: "Let now the astrologers, the stargazers, the monthly prognosticators, stand up and save thee from these things that shall come upon thee. Behold they shall be as stubble; the fire shall burn them; they shall not deliver themselves from the power of the flame."

According to the Bible astrology is pagan idol worship, blasphemy, apostasy from the living God. The First Commandment has been forgotten: "Thou shalt not make unto thee any graven image, or any likeness of anything that is in heaven above, or that is in the earth beneath or that is in the water under the earth."

## II. CARTOMANCY

Historically, fortune-telling from cards can be traced over many centuries. The Romans already possessed a system of little tablets with inscribed symbols. Then in the 8th century cards appeared. The technique of fortune-telling from cards is rather simple. Certain cards have certain meanings, for instance 7 of hearts: card of love; 10 of hearts: fulfilled wish; 10 of spades: lucky card. With 32 playing cards there are thousands of combinations. Let us get acquainted with some of the main problems of fortune-telling from cards through some examples.

E 6 An evangelist of the German Tent Mission gave a lecture against fortune-telling and card laying. Afterwards a church official who was present called the evangelist to account and told him: "What do you mean by this protest against card laying? I do it myself. It is a harmless social game." — To this example from Germany follows a similar one from Switzerland.

E 7 A Swiss minister held a bazaar. In the parish hall several fairy-tale booths were erected. One of the booths had the inscription: "Fortunes Told". For 20 Rappen the children could enter this booth and get their fortunes told by a fortune-telling woman. A church elder grew indignant about this and told the minister. "This is a harmless joke", said the minister. A boy who entered this ecclesiastical fortune-telling booth received the information: "You will crash with your bicycle next week." Several days later he actually had a spill. The boy broke his leg. A girl received this fortune: "The teacher does not like you." Since that time the girl suffered much from this alleged dislike of her teacher.

These first two examples show that fortune-telling from cards cannot be called harmless. The two children became victims of a suggestion. The two ministers were victims of their rationalistic humbug theory of their university education, which leaves a disastrous gap in the field of magic (mastery of matter through the mind or soul) and mantic (art of fortune-telling).

2. If card laying is not only concerned with making easy money, but paranormal (extraordinary) abilities play a part, then telepathy (reading of thoughts, tapping of thoughts) and subconscious communication (intimation, connection) plays a role. An example shall make this clear.

E 8   A sixteen year old girl went to a card laying fortune-teller. She wanted to know how long she would have to wait till the longed-for suitor would appear. The fortune-telling woman looked at her closely and said: "Your brother had a serious motorcycle accident a year ago. Is that true?" "Yes." "Your mother has heart trouble. Is that true?" "Yes." "At present you have trouble with your father. Is that true?" "Yes, but how do you know all this?" "From the cards." In reality the fortune-telling woman possessed the rare ability of telepathy (reading of thoughts) and therefore read these statements from the girl. Because of this information the young client put her full confidence in this fortune-teller. Now the woman gave her informations about the future. The girl believed the ambiguous statements and adjusted herself inwardly. In her superstition she fell victim to a fulfilment compulsion. The Word of the Bible was applicable here: "According to your faith be it done unto you." The accurately told past triggered the psychological process of unconsciously-caused fulfilment.

3. Another form of card laying is based on genuine mediumistic abilities. The word mediu-

mistic comes from the Latin medium. With mediumistic one defines mysterious abilities of some
people to produce or to lay hold on occurrences, that
seem to transcend the range of the five senses. Let
us listen to a card laying woman with mediumistic
abilities.

E 9  In reply to questions a fortune-telling woman
declared, that in the moment of fortune-telling she
was ruled by a strange power. A foreign spirit
would come over her. She had to say things then
which she did not know herself. She had the feeling
as if she was possessed in the moment of fortune-
telling. Afterwards she was completely normal
again.

With this example we are in the area of the
example in Acts 16, 16—18. Paul was on a missionary journey in Philippi. A fortune-telling woman crossed his way. Daily she called in the streets
to the crowds: "These men are the servants of the
most high God, which show unto us the way of
salvation." Should not Paul have rejoiced about this
affirmation? Why did he restrain this woman? The
Apostle saw immediately that here fortune-telling
powers from below were at work. In the Name of
Jesus he confronted this woman and commanded:
"In the Name of Jesus Christ come out of her."
Immediately the woman was freed of her fortune-
telling ability. This incident in this young mission
to Europe is very enlightening. First of all we learn
that there are genuine fortune-telling powers and

not everything is swindle and humbug. The woman told true facts. She received her knowledge from outer-human intelligences, from demonic powers. Further it becomes clear that fortune-telling also gives out pious contents. Only too often the occult (dark, demonic) doings of such people are camouflaged with Christian trimmings. The Apostle immediately recognized the source of this fortune-telling ability. He had the gift of proving and discerning of spiritis. Immediately his spiritual authority in his missionary ministry was revealed. The Name of Jesus was equal to all the dark doings of the world of darkness. The whole victory of the Gospel over the demon-bound pagan world rose radiantly. In the Name of Jesus the chains and fetters broke. The poor, tormented human being was set free. — The manifold facts in this story appear again and again in many variations in fortune-telling.

4. Christian counseling is not interested in the scientific issues but in the effects of fortune-telling and how to overcome them. Several examples shall make this clear.

E 10   During a counseling session a student reported different psychic disturbances. She had a fear of exams, symptoms of paralysis and no power to concentrate on her work. She gave the impression as if her intellectual and emotional faculties were split. In reply to questions she admitted that she often had her fortune told from cards. Her ancestors too had been advised by fortune-tellers.

E 11   For many years a Christian university graduate practiced card laying for himself and his family, also for fellow church members. After his death his wife became an alcoholic. Her whole pension went for liquor. A battery of bottles decorated her house. Together with this evil the woman engaged in white magic and thus continued in the occult tradition of her husband. The daughter followed in the footsteps of her parents. She was also caught in the superstitious customs of her mother. When the girl was seventeen years old she became mentally ill. She was committed to an insane asylum. Magic and superstition had destroyed this whole family.

E 12   A young Christian man told me about his time in the service. He was a corporal in a unit where the staff sergeant laid cards for all NCO's. At first the corporal objected to this fortune-telling. Finally he gave in to his superior. The card layer prophecied to him that the next day he would receive news of a death. He also could expect a money-order during the next days. As a matter of fact the following day he received the news that his uncle had died. Five days later he also received the announced money. The parents were never in the habit of sending their son money. It was a singular happening. After this session with the card layer, the corporal experienced depressions (melancholy thoughts). His prayer life was disturbed. He consulted a Christian man for counseling help. After the man prayed and laid hands on him the serious emotional disturbance disappeared completely.

These examples deal with a number of problems. The simplest complex of questions are the parapsychological or psychological questions (Parapsychology - science of the extraordinary border experiences of life). Did the staff sergeant possess genuine fortune-telling abilities? In the above example E 12 it is not evident. The corporal could have known of the serious illness of his uncle. Besides he could have played with the idea of his parents sending him some money as a congratulatory gift for his recent promotion. Then the staff sergeant, with the help of a special sensitivity or telepathic faculty to put himself in the place of the other person, could have tapped the information from the corporal. This does not seem at all like a case of genuine prevision.

The second group of questions have medical character. Were these disturbances caused or triggered by fortune-telling? Was this not rather a latent (hidden) emotional or even mental illness that came to the surface at the time of the fortune-telling experience? Is not the timely coincidence erroneously taken as the cause? Is not the cause therefore being mistaken for the effect? These are the objections that are always being raised by psychiatry (science of mental and emotional illnesses). Behind these medical objections are weighty Biblical, theological problems. Medicine widely contests, and so do many theologians, that occult practice can evoke psychic, nervous disturbances and damages to the life of faith. A further step back lies the problem whether there are outer-human, demonic powers whose operations reach into human life. In this connection the psychiatrists, almost without exception, view the New Testament reports about the possessed to be cases of serious hysteria. Many theologians follow along this line, and speak of possession as of a disease or a defect. First there are those theologians who have not managed to get rid of the rationalistic egg-shells of their liberal theology, especially all adherents of Bultmann's theology. They miss the true facts of the Biblical report entirely. They do not have an organ of receptivity to Biblical happenings. Spiritual whoredom with the philosophical trends of the past and present has blunted them against the pneuma (the Holy Spirit). It is indeed embarrassing, when even a positive theologian from Basel, who develops good New Testament thoughts in her booklet "Salvation and Healing", calls fortune-telling ability a defect. This is the influence of psychiatric doubts. Principally in the New Testament defects or diseases are being healed, but the possessed are being commanded in the Name of Jesus. The fortune-teller woman in Philippi had no defect, but a demonic spirit from below. Therefore Paul did not heal her by laying on of hands and prayer, but he commanded in the Name of Jesus that the unclean spirits should come out of her. The therapy which Jesus and his Apostles used makes it clear what the patient was suffering from. To the physically sick laying on of hands and prayer was applied, while the unclean spirits and demons were met with the authority of the casting-out command.

If we return now to the medical questions of the beginning, we see that the view of the Bible is at variance with the view of psychiatry. Of course it is conceded to medicine that many mental illnesses have a magical factor or complex. This is apparent in many conversations with schizophrenics who often assert that they are magically persecuted or bewitched. With this observation the other fact must not be devaluated, that in many cases magic is the primary cause and psychic disturbances are effects and consequences. 3000 carefully examined cases are a weighty evidence. Besides our parapsychologists, for instance Dr. Bender of the University of Freiburg, know about diseases which started after occult practice. Mediumistic psychosis needs only to be mentioned. Christian counseling shows plainly that spiritistic, magic or fortune-telling activity brings on disturbances, which can often be shown medically. But in almost every case damages to the life of faith can be pointed out. This observation indicates that the origin of these damages rests first of all on Biblical grounds. For their treatment the theological counselor, if he is a Bible believing Christian, is chiefly qualified, and next to him a believing psychiatrist.

## III. PALMISTRY

To avoid mistakes, some concepts have to be cleared up. This chapter deals with chiromancy, fortune-telling from the lines of the hand. Chirology the scientific interpretation of hand shape and hand line, is not to be considered. Also graphology, the interpretation of hand writing is not to be discussed.

Palmistry can be traced back to ancient Rome. Early astrological ideas were mixed into palmistry. Beside the four main lines (heart, head, fate and life line) the palm is divided into seven planet mounds. From the index finger to the little finger they are: Mercury, Apollo, Saturn and Jupiter mound. Below the thumb is the Venus mound, under the little finger the Mars and Moon mound.

1. A few examples shall again introduce the questions of Christian counseling. When it was mentioned above that definitionally chiromancy, chirology and graphology must be kept seperate, in practice often a disastrous mixing takes place. First an example of this kind.

E 13   A young girl went to a graphologist and had her handwriting and her hand lines interpreted. In the written account it was stated that she would be murdered in her 30th year. Thereupon the girl declared to her family: "If I have to die so young,

I want to enjoy my life to the fullest." She engaged in prostitution and committed abortion. Because of her dissolute life, she got sick in her 24th year and died of ulcerative colitis. The doctor himself stated that she had ruined herself with her licentious manner of life. It is noteworthy that after the session with the graphologist, mediumistic abilities had appeared in the girl. She could use the pendulum and divining rod.

This example shows first that this graphologist was an occult practitioner. He misused graphology for purposes of fortune-telling. Also the most frequent form of palmistry and fortune-telling is revealed here. There are many forms of suggestive fortune-telling. The person who has been advised by fortune-tellers brings about the fulfilment consciously or unconsciously. Here is a repetition of what has been said about the psychological process of card laying. In regard to Christian counseling, it is observed frequently that fortune-telling causes people to feel no moral inhibitions. Christian education, tradition and custom have thrown up protective dams around all our lives. Even the person who is far from Christ, lives unconsciously in the Christian world order, though he may rebel against it inwardly. Taking hold of occult powers tears down these dams. Dark, turbid floods stream openly into the abandoned life. In our case, the sensual life of the girl wins the upper hand. She is ruined by it. Occultism encourages all passions and addictions. The occultly advised person in many cases becomes irascible, abandoned to alcohol, nicotine and a licentious life.

The effects of fortune-telling suggestions are shown in the following examples.

E 14   A young woman had her fortune told through palmistry. The fortune-teller told her that in her fortieth year she would have cancer and die. As a matter of fact the woman grew thin before her fortieth birthday because of this suggestion and since that time she is living under the delusion that she is going to have cancer. She lost already 30 pounds and weighs only 84 pounds.

E 15   The cousin of one of my class mates was working as a maid in a manse. One day a gypsy appeared at the door to sell household articles. The girl refused to buy anything because of the high prices. Thereupon the gypsy grabbed the hand of the girl to tell her fortune. The girl wanted to pull her hand back when the sly woman used a psychological trick. She said quickly: "Oh, how interesting. You will marry in two  years." Which girl does not listen when marriage is promised to her? Willingly she let the gypsy read her hand. She continued with her prophecy: "Several suitors will come. You will marry the tallest one. In your first year of marriage you will become a mother. As a matter of fact your life line stops quite suddenly. You will die during the birth of your first child."

Before the report is being continued, the character of this fortune-telling shall be pointed out briefly. Certainly no prophetic ability was necessary to prophesy a beautiful girl that she would marry. Besides one would not have to be a prophet to tell her that in her first year of marriage she would become a mother. The dark ending with the death announcement was certainly only an act of vengeance by the gypsy, because nothing had been bought from her. This is not genuine fortune-telling but only primitive suggestive fortune-telling. How did this prophecy work out?

Actually several suitors appeared in the following two years. The girl stood already under the influence of the prophecy. She married the tallest one. In the course of the first year she felt she was going to be a mother. The closer the hour of delivery came the greater grew her fear. She struggled with the dark prophecy. Her relatives and especially her husband tried to dissuade her from believing this nonsense. They did not succeed. The young woman did not have a strong enough faith to develop a right counter-balance against the superstition. She had a normal delivery. Several days later she got a high fever. The physician declared that there was no organic cause at all for this fever. Three weeks after the delivery she became mentally deranged. She was taken to a psychiatrc clinic, where she died after three days.

Only one who does not know the psychology of fortune-telling will call this a true prophecy. In all probability this is a suggestion. We know from our mission fields that pagan natives are completely dependent on the prophecies of their medicine men and magic priests. When a tribal magician predicts the date of death to a member of his tribe, then this prediction comes true promptly. One speaks here of the psychological phenomenon of thanatomania, the seeking of death. There is a death by suggestion, and not only with the primitive people, but also with the civilized Europeans. In this connection Americans have made experiments with convicts that have given positive proof. A man who had been convicted to death was blindfolded. He was told that he was to die by having the main artery at his neck opened. In one minute he would be dead. The skin of his neck was superficially scratched, and at the same time a faucet was turned on near by. The convict felt the cut and heard the splashing of the water. In one minute he lost consciousness. The trick was a success.

2. In regard to the contents of fortune-telling and the form of the prophecies, Professor Zucker in his 'Psychology of Superstition' distinguishes between magical and mystical superstition and as a third form presentiment. Magical superstition is active. It puts into operation suggestive and magical powers. It sets to work decisively and formatively in the life of the one who seeks advice. Almost all of the examples so far lie on this level. Mystical superstition has intuitive, adaptive character. It

works with intuition, meditation and sensitivity. To it belongs the ability of combination, of tapping, adaptation and assimilation. There is a principle in magic superstition that the ego masters the world, so in mystical superstition the ego becomes merged with the world. The practice of tapping distinguishes basically between two different kinds. One says timely prevision has two possibilities. Either man who is supposed to carry within himself his whole future in rudiments (traces, points of beginning) is being tapped. Or a plan-carrying subject i.e. a world consciousness is supposed to exist, which carries in itself all plans for the fate of all people. That is the opinion of Prof. Osty, E. von Hartmann and Prof. Driesch. This plan-carrying subject could be tapped by medias. Both views are based on a certain determinism (predestination). From the Biblical point of view these two techniques of fortune-telling are not acceptable. To the third group of presentiment belong the unconsciously arising premonitions, monitions, veridical dreams, experiences of second sight, phenomena of clairvoyance, in fact all effects of mediumistic abilities. A good example of this kind is to be found in the diamond example in "Seelsorge und Okkultismus" (Ist edit. page 73; 2nd edit. page 69) I do not want to repeat it here in order not to overlap the different publications.

3. Of more importance than all scientific differentiations as interesting as they may be, are the concerns of Christian counseling. Mentally and emo-

tionally disturbed people have to be helped whose symptoms do not fit into the psychiatric picture. To show the effects of palmistry two more examples shall be added.

E 16   A woman fortune-teller strictly rejected all divine things. One day a Christian girl got acquainted with her. When she heard about her strange fortune-telling business she jokingly held out her hand. She thought it was all silly nonsense. The woman read her palm. The girl could not withhold a mocking remark and laughed merrily. Afterwards the Christian girl suffered from depressions and could no longer believe. The children of the woman fortune-teller also showed the typical effects. They all are neurotics and live immoral lives. Here, too, are shown the typical characteristics of the effects: depressions and loss of inhibition.

E 17   For many years a man actively engaged in palmistry. Besides he was a practicing mesmerist. Through the years he personally felt the destructive influence of his dubious occupation. He wanted to turn to Christ and to the Word of God. Many months he forced himself to read the Bible, though he felt a strong inner resistance. Each time when he met with divine things he felt a strange inward defence and strong pressure.

A new aspect is shown in this example. Fortune-telling develops the phenomenon of resistance, the inner defence against all divine things. When a person who has engaged in fortune-telling wants to come to Christ, he cannot believe. Violent, sinister, defensive forces appear which want to prevent a decision for Christ. The person who has been infected and 'immunized' by fortune-telling, is nearly almost insensitive against the Holy Spirit. For such people it is very difficult to turn to Christ.

## IV. DIVINING ROD AND PENDULUM

As many other occult practices, so the pendulum practice tries to become scientifically acceptable. One developed radiaesthesis, science of radiation, and asserts that all matter radiates. The dowser or pendulum practitioner is supposed to be able to feel himself into these rays. The scientific aspect of this problem is discussed in "Seelsorge und Okkultismus" page 84, resp. 81. This book is concerned with practical questions of Christian counseling. In order not to confuse the unacquainted, it must be said that the same processes are being laid hold of with the divining rod and the pendulum. The pendulum is only supposed to be the more delicate indicator. To make an objective judgment possible, first examples with no apparent ill effects are given.

1. There are physicians, ministers, missionaries and engineers who are convinced of the usefulness and exactness of the pendulum claims (results from rod and pendulum). They declare that except for a

certain weakening of nervous energy they feel no derogatory effects.

E 18    A 28 year old man committed suicide. Since his body could not be found, the police searched for it. His brother-in-law consulted a pendulum practitioner. He asked for an object of the dead man. He was given some stockings. The pendulum practitioner laid the stockings on the floor and walked around them rectangularly with a metal rod. Then he correctly identified the dead man. He stated his name, date of birth and the place where the body was supposed to be. Then additionally he checked his own statements by taking a map and using the pendulum again to find the place where the body was located. The pendulum verified the account of the rod. The brother-in-law went to the specified place with the police and actually found the body in the determined place. The man had shot himself in a little shed in the forest.

E 19    A physician from Alsace is a dowser. He considers this ability as a gift of God. Noteworthy though is his defensive attitude against all divine things and his nervousness.

E 20    A postal employee has the ability to search for water veins with the divining rod and pendulum, also to identify correctly the position of postal cables with the pendulum. He also speaks of signs of weariness after dowsing.

E 21    A physician had a house built for himself. He wanted to have a well in his garden. A friend of his, a Protestant minister, heard of his desire. He asked the doctor to give him a ground-plan of house and garden. Then he took the pendulum and established on the plan the place where water was to be found. His designations were correct. After digging there water was found.

E 22  A missionary has the ability to establish with the pendulum from the second story of a house, whether downstairs on the first floor a male or female person has entered the house. He can also determine through the walls, if for instance the female person downstairs expects a child and of what sex that child will be. In the presence of his friends he made many such experiments, all of them successful. In the same way he can identify graves in a grave-yard, whether a male or female person lies under the tombstone. Naturally he stands behind the stone, so he cannot read the name.

E 23  A Salvation Army officer was a pendulum practitioner for many years. During the war, when his son was missing, he used the pendulum over his son's photo, to determine whether the son was still alive. When in the post-war period his suitcase was stolen, he used the pendulum to identify the place where the stolen suitcase was. The pendulum indicated the right place. My question, whether he felt any derogatory effects of his pendulum practice was denied by this kingdom worker. He declared, he felt that no damage was done to his life of faith.

Glancing quickly over these five examples they

furnish us already with a few clues from which to form an opinion. First of all it becomes clear that these things cannot be explained away with the humbug theory. There are dowsers and pendulum practitioners which can make exact statements, even though many geologists and other scientists passionately debate it. It must not be overlooked of course, that there are many statements from pendulum practitioners which only contain confused, muddled, good-for-nothing stuff.

Furthermore it appears from the few examples that dowsing and pendulum practice is a strongly contested field. Here physicians, ministers, missionaries and government employees are named who work with the pendulum. Whose side is right then? The fanatical supporters or the passionate combatants? The following argument is wrong: If ministers and other kingdom workers use the pendulum, then it must be a harmless thing. Even so we cannot say that adultery is allowed, because a missionary has committed adultery. The following reasoning also is disputable: When some kingdom workers do not feel any derogatory effects from the use of the pendulum, then an opposite observation would be of no importance. Indeed I know of cases where dowsing with divining rods had apparently no ill effects on the dowser. But it must not be kept secret that effects also can remain latent. With some people the cloven foot shows itself only on the deathbed or maybe sooner when they want to come to Christ. We also have to be freed from the notion, that everyone who proclaims the Word of God is a Christian. The Word of Holy Scripture is still applicable: "They preach, and I did not send them" (Romans 10, 15) A minister who uses the pendulum can be equally subjected as one who belongs to a different professional group. Through many cases from my counseling practice I observed that the Catholic priest Emmenegger who used the pendulum on his patients, in many cases passed on serious subjections to his clients. Recently a Protestant minister also was tried and found guilty of serious offences during a treatment by pendulum.

Disastrous confusion is brought about by the idea that the ability to use the pendulum is a gift of God. It is not only the opinion of the mentioned Alsatian doctor but also of some ministers. Is this right? The examination of many family histories shows that dowsing ability, reaction to the pendulum, mesmerism, clairvoyance, ability of second sight and veridical dreams occur in such persons whose line of ancestors included a magic charmer or active spiritist. These unusual human faculties are therefore not gifts of the Spirit (charismata) nor even neutral, natural gifts, but mediumistic faculties. There are many people who possess these faculties without being conscious of them. Sometimes they are detected accidentally. Once in a while the curious thing happens that such a possessor of mediumistic faculties gets saved and comes to Christ. Suddenly in following Christ he discovers his extraordinary abilities and is then of the opinion that he has a gift of the Spirit. That is of course a deception. In Christian counseling one makes the following observation: Sometimes these mediumistic faculties disappear when that person becomes converted. But often they are being dragged into the new life. If a follower of Jesus prays seriously to be delivered from these faculties, then his prayer will be answered. To many Christians these faculties are burdensome. Markus Hauser declared, that clairvoyance was to him a plague not a gift. Never must these mediumistic faculties be regarded as gifts of the Spirit. Mediumistic faculties are not even sanctified through conversion. What has been acquired in the service of Satan by the ancestors will not be taken over and sanctioned by the Holy Spirit.

2. The connection between use of the pendulum and mediumistic abilities shall be made clear with two examples.

E 24 A young man was being treated for a disease by a nature healer who also was a pendulum practitioner and practiced magic charming. After the treatment the patient developed mediumistic faculties. Suddenly he was clairvoyant and developed the faculty of mental suggestion at a distance.

E 25 After the war a woman gave her missing husband's photo to a pendulum practitioner in order for him to find him. Afterwards she experienced symptoms of clairvoyance. She had somnambulistic experiences. She could send out her soul, as it were, over great distances. In her distress she came for Christian counseling. After she confessed and surrendered her life to Christ, these mediumistic faculties again disappeared.

There are conscious and unconscious transmittances of mediumistic faculties. Through treatment by a highly mediumistic occultist, the treated patient easily becomes mediumistic himself. We have here the demonic counterpart to the laying on of hands of the disciples in Acts. Through the Apostles' laying on of hands many Christians received the gift of the Holy Spirit (Acts 8, 17; 19, 6). There are also conscious transmittances with dowsers and pendulum practitioners. In counseling many said that they had received the sensitivity to the divining rod from a strong dowser holding their hand while searching for water. Then suddenly the rod had reacted in their hand also. This mediumistic faculty stayed with them also afterwards.

3. Following are some examples which, better than all theory give an insight into the tension-packed problem of the mediumistic faculties and the spiritual, Biblical powers.

E 26   A woman who had an organic disease went to a pendulum practitioner to be examined. Diagnosis and determination of medicine was made with the pendulum. The woman who had a Christian background afterwards felt approached by sinister forces. These strange assaults lasted a few months. During this time when she experienced these strange feelings of fear, she came for Christian counseling.

E 27  A girl from childhood on had the faculty of second sight. She often saw apparitions. She strongly rejected divine things. During an evangelization she received Christ as her Savior. From this moment on all resistance against divine things was gone. During an illness she unknowingly went to a pendulum practitioner. Immediately her psychic disturbances and her resistance against God's Word and prayer returned.

This example confirms the following facts. It has been said earlier that the faculty of second sight belongs to the magic subsequent effects of occult practices of the ancestors. A companion symptom of these magic subsequent effects is also often resistance against all divine things. The girl in E 27 had both symptoms. After she turned to Christ the mediumistic subjection left. After the pendulum treatment both of them appeared again. Here the mediumistic character of the pendulum practice becomes apparent. The characteristic of resistance as companion symptom shall be made clear on other examples.

E 28  During an illness a woman sought help from a widely known pendulum practitioner. She thought nothing cf it, and up to that time she had not heard anything derogatory about diagnosis by pendulum. In the waiting room of the pendulum practitioner she became restless inwardly. This unrest increased during the treatment itself. She took the medicines which had been determined by the pendulum. The degree of her psychic disturbances intensified. She could no longer pray, had an aversion to the Word of God and experienced an ever growing disgust with divine things. Without anyone advising her, on her own initiative she finally threw away the medicines. Only then she came for Christian counseling and asked me what I thought about diagnosis and determination of medicines by pendulum.

E 29   A pendulum practitioner sought my Christian counsel. He admitted quite frankly that the pendulum practice was a strain that consumed his nervous energy. He specialized in determining the salubrity of foods with the pendulum. He declared that white sugar would affect him negatively, brown sugar positively. After heating honey over 140° it was also positive. Through the years he observed on himself psychic changes. He suffered loss of energy and the power to make decisions. He developed a tremendous sensitivity. Nervous twitching and sensitivity to South wind and water appeared. When he tried to read the Bible he had a feeling of disgust and a great aversion. Crucifixes were also violently repugnant to him. Since he personally observed that these psychic-religious disturbances were connected with his pendulum practice, he sought help in Christian counseling and was ready to surrender his life to Christ.

In these two examples it is shown that the woman as well as the pendulum practitioner became aware of the derogatory effects through a healthy feeling and clear observation. They came to reject it before they received such advice from the Christian counselor.

The opposition of the mediumistic pendulum practice to the spiritual power of prayer shall be shown in three examples.

E 30   A well-known dowser was asked by a professor of medicine one day to walk through the different buildings of the clinic with the divining rod and note the reactions of the rod. The reason for the professor's request was the observation, that in one of the houses of the clinic a specially high rate of deaths occurred. When seriously ill people were moved to this house, their condition usually took a turn for the worse. But the professor did not tell this to the dowser. He wanted to have an unbiased report. The dowser went through the different buildings and actually established that there were stronger impulses in the 'death house'. The professor who did not believe in the rod phenomena had screening boxes built in to complete the experiment. The success was baffling. Immediately the number of deaths declined. In order not to be talked about by his colleagues, the professor is usually silent about this experiment.

This dowser possessed next to the sensitivity to the divining rod also the ability of clairvoyance. He can state at any time where the members of his family are. He also is consulted by insurance companies and real estate agents to determine the condition of building lots. In the course of his activities this dowser and clairvoyant declared that he could no longer pray. An inner force was hindering him from it.

E 31 A Christian park owner wanted to locate a spring in his garden. A dowser found reactions in two places of the park. The digging proved unsuccessful. Thereupon the dowser declared: "This has never happened to me." The park owner answered: "I prayed about it, because I was not sure, whether I as a Christian could call a dowser." The dowser answered: "Well, that's why; then of course it won't work."

E 32 A pendulum practitioner speaks charms over warts, corns, goitres, excemas etc. Moreover he experiments in the field of death magic. He also asserts that he can make people sick and well. A believing woman who knew nothing of his magic and thought him only to be a nature healer, came to him for treatment. In the waiting room she prayed silently. Suddenly he addressed her: "You can go home, I cannot help you." In spite of this, from this hour on the woman had attacks of depression and thoughts of suicide. Her husband who had no clear relationship to Christ, was treated magically by this same pendulum practitioner. The children which were born to his wife after this treatment are subjected. It is strange that a physician sends difficult patients to this pendulum practitioner.

These three examples show that dowsing paralyzed this man's desire to pray. On the other hand the prayer of the believing Christian made dowsing impossible. The praying woman in the waiting room paralyzed the activity of the magic pendulum practitioner. Pneuma (Holy Spirit) and mediumistic faculties (application of occult powers) are mutually exclusive.

4. A special paragraph shall be devoted to the effects of the pendulum practice. They do not deal with damages to the life of faith, but with medically authenticated disturbances.

E 33    A young, unemployed man had a pendulum practitioner find jobs for him by using the pendulum over the 'Help Wanted' collumn. With the help of this man he received five job offerings in one day. He got a job immediately, but after a few days he had to give it up again because he became emotionally disturbed. He spent a few months in a mental hospital. After he improved he turned to some monks who advised him again with the help of the pendulum. Finally he was advised by a magic charmer. The result was that a few days later he had attacks of frenzy and was taken again to the mental hospital.

E 34  A young man with bronchial asthma was being treated by a pendulum practitioner. Diagnosis and right medicine was determined with the pendulum. Besides being a pendulum practitioner he also was a magic charmer. On the young man with bronchial asthma he used the following charm: "Blood turn to water, water turn to pus, pus come out." Then he put band-aids on several parts of his body. The band-aids were covered with a salve. Actually after a few days pus had formed under the band-aids. The pus drained but the bronchial asthma had not been healed. But from this time on the young man had nervous and mental disturbances. He felt that his memory was failing, he could concentrate no longer on his studies and he felt a numbness in his head. These disturbances caused him to seek Christian counsel.

E 35  A Protestant preacher used the pendulum to find water and ore. He also diagnosed diseases and established the salubrity of medicines with the pendulum. A Swiss university professor examined his ability. In the presence of his medical assistants and students he introduced twenty patients to the pendulum practitioner. With the help of the pendulum the man made a right diagnosis on all 20 patients. This preacher also was not spared from the effects of the pendulum practice. His wife had a fatal accident. All of his children died an unnatural death. He himself has been in an insane asylum for a year.

E 36  A minister in Middle Germany used the

pendulum to find out diseases and medicines. He also practiced healings over distance. The sick sent him their photos. He used the pendulum over the photo and found out the right medicines for the diseases. A believing Christian woman also sent him her photo to be treated by him. She received the diagnosis and medicine. Later on she became insane and was taken to the insane asylum. Members of her family reported it to the church officials. The minister was called to account.

These four examples from Christian counseling show the fact which has been observed a hundred-fold, that the pendulum therapy can accomplish certain relief and healings in the organic field. This organic relief must be paid for with disturbances in the psychic field. Even the preacher who was an active pendulum practitioner was not spared by it. The degree of psychic sickness differs only in this way, that the active pendulum practitioner experiences more complicated sicknesses as result of his mediumistic activity than the passively treated. In many cases the occult character of the pendulum practice is revealed by the fact, that the pendulum practitioner often practices other occult activities, like magic charming, spiritism, clairvoyance, mesmerism etc. The pendulum practice is in good company. Birds of a feather flock together.

# V. MIRROR MANTIC

There are occult instruction books about mirror mantic and mirror magic. The mirror magician, with the help of a magic mirror, wants to conduct treatment by distance, healings, persecution magic, warding-off magic, love magic and other magical practices. Mirror mantic, with the help of a mirror, wants to find hidden things, uncover crimes, diagnose difficult diseases, recognize physical occurrences in the cosmos and other things. As occult tools not only magic mirrors are used but also crystal balls, rock crystal and other reflecting objects. Some even use the reflection of water in this way.

Historically, mirror or crystal gazing can be traced over hundreds of years. Even in the fairy tale with the mirror on the wall this motive is found. Mirror gazing also has its place in mysticism. Jacob Boehme is supposed to have received his best thoughts while meditating over the cobbler's ball. From the psychological point of view crystal gazing may be a help for auto-suggestion or auto-hypnosis and for the release of subconscious processes. This indicates that in this form of fortune-telling mainly subconscious forces are put into action. Since these subconscious forces widely withdraw themselves from conscious control, they can also be the entrance door for outer-human forces. Paul does not say in vain that we do not wrestle against flesh and blood, but against the evil spirits of the air. (Eph. 6, 12)

A few examples shall introduce this form of fortune-telling.

E 37   A big farmer owned many sheep. One day several of them had disappeared and could not be found. The boy ran to the miracle doctor, who with the help of his mirror could solve and clear all mysteries, and he asked him for advice. The crystal gazer went into his chamber and stayed there for quite a while. Finally he appeared again and gave the following information: "Go out to the first road, then turn to the right and climb staight up the mountain. On the highest summit lies a big rock. Next to this rock are the lost sheep." The boy followed his advice and found the sheep.

E 38   A farmer from the Kappler valley comes to the crystal gazer and laments: "This night my cow has been stolen. Can you tell me where she is?" The mirror gazer goes into his chamber and concentrates on his mirror. Finally he comes out and states: "Your cow is on Holzerjoerg's farm. In fact she is hidden in the barn behind a few bundles of straw. Take three or four people along and the sheriff. Half of you go into the house and the other half go right into the barn." The man followed this advice and found his cow.

E 39   One night the garage including the car of a non-Christian man burned down. Since he assumed it to be arson he notified the police. The police investigation was without success. To identify the arsonist, he went to a man who practiced mirror magic. The clairvoyant retreated for about twenty minutes into his chamber. Then he stepped out of the half-darkened room and held his magic mirror before the man and said: "This is the arsonist." The startled man recognized in the mirror his former schoolmate and exclaimed: "This is not possible. We are on very good terms." The clairvoyant declared: "The mirror does not lie." While leaving, the clairvoyant said quite incidentally: "Besides you will die soon." The bewildered man now went to see his schoolmate, looked into his eyes and asked him: "Did you have something to do with the burning of my garage?" The schoolmate became quite confused and actually admitted the arson. In reply to questions about the motive, the arsonist admitted that he was jealous of his business success, since he himself always suffered reverses in his profession. The arsonist then begged his victim to keep silent about this. He wanted to replace the garage and car, which he did presently.

About four weeks after this meeting with the clairvoyant, one night the victim of the arsonist screamed terribly. His wife awoke from the scream, turned on the light and saw her husband writhing in terrible convulsions. She got the doctor immediately, who had the seriously ill man transferred to the university clinic. He remained unconscious from the experience of the night and had to be fed intravenously for ten days. During this time of unconsciousness, a church group interceded for him daily. Finally the patient regained consciousness and reported what he had experienced daily during these ten days. When in the beginning of his strange sickness he had cried out in the night, he saw in a dream or half-dream horrible, devilish figures approaching, which pulled him along on a descent into hell. During this strange experience all the guilt of his life appeared before his eyes. He also recognized the minute details of the arson, the session with the clairvoyant came also to life again. The black figures that dragged him into the dark abyss explained to him that the measure of his sins was full, and he now had to be crucified for them. He experienced a terribly painful crucifixion. After horrible mistreatments and seemingly unending torments these black figures disappeared again. It got lighter about him, he regained consciousness. Later he heard from the doctor that he had been unconscious for 10 days. After this experience the arsonist's victim was completely changed. The man who had formerly not wanted to hear anything of the Word of God began to attend the worship service and Bible hours of the church faithfully. He became so active that on Sundays he filled his car with neighbors and drove them to Sunday School.

Beside all confused and doubtful statements of many mirror fortune-tellers, these three examples show the useful results of this mirror information. In the first two cases I was not able to follow up the effects of mirror counseling. The third example clearly shows the effects. Assumedly the man fell victim to a subliminal suggestion, as the fortune-teller stated incidentally: "Besides you will die soon." The arson victim had been much disturbed by the disclosure that his schoolmate had been the arsonist. His thoughts concentrated on the man and the ignominious story. At this moment his conciousness was diverted and his subconscious was open. This was the favourable moment for the mirror practitioner to work in his suggestion, which then reached the subconscious. The sickness is probably the effect of this subliminal suggestion. This is not true prevision. It was therefore, to use the terminology of Zucker, no mystical or foreseeing fortune-telling act, but a magic, an influencing fortune-telling act. Such examples are sufficient to the Christian counselor to warn of any form of fortune-telling.

## VI. PSYCHOMETRY

The word psychometry means 'to measure the soul'. The definition was originally used by the American professor Buchanan. It is extremely difficult to state the essence of psychometry. A few examples may introduce the matter better.

E 40   A young man who came to me for Christian counseling has the strange ability to identify with the help of an object the particulars and peculiarities of a respective person. One case shall be reported here. One day he received from the family physician, who wanted to test him, a few handwritten lines. The doctor did not state whose handwriting sample this was. The boy concentrated on the lines and then made exact statements as to the writer, her address, her family background, her diseases and other things. The doctor verified the truth of these statements.

In this example the question appears whether it was not just simple telepathy. Maybe this young clairvoyant did not get these statements from the handwriting sample but from the physician. At best this argument can prove only partly right, for some things were said which the doctor did not know, but which he found later to be correct.

E 41 During an evangelization in Switzerland I met a clairvoyant through Christian counseling, who works psychometrically and can make 100% true statements. If one puts before him an object of a patient who is unknown to him, for example a handkerchief, he is able to identify the disease of the respective person. A professor in Zurich examined this ability and confirmed the reliability of the statements.

I know of other psychometric acts of this clairvoyant. In the same way he can state what diseases people have died from. — Another psychometric example is reported in E 18.

The difficult question is how this psychometric clairvoyance comes about. Some parapsychologists like Richet, Geley, Osty, Price, Gumppenberg, Gatterer, think that clothing and all objects of daily use become impregnated by the individual. The psychometric clairvoyant is supposed to have the ability to take hold of and to interpret these mental-psychic impressions. This explanation becomes very questionable, when one considers, that the psychometric clairvoyant with the help of an object is not only able to state the past, but also the future of the respective person. Without doubt we are here in the field of mediumistic fortune-telling. This supposition ist being confirmed when one examines the fate of the psychometrists. In Christian counseling I had the opportunity to examine psychometric practices. The clairvoyant in E 40 for instance wanted to come to Christ. At this moment the phenomenon of pronounced resistance developed. Resistance against all divine things became so tremendous, that in the moment of prayer his thought concentration vanished. Afterwards his mind was completely clear again. It was not even possible for him to repeat a prayer, although he is an intelligent man and wanted to pray. No encouragement from the Word of God penetrated this wall. During prayer he had fainting spells. Later I found out that this psychometrist was also using the dangerous magic book, the 6th and 7th Book of Moses. This circumstance is characteristic again of the mediumistic character of psychometry: psychometry in company of black magic.

There are still other forms of fortune-telling to be discussed, for instance fortune-telling based on excursion of the psyche. Also to this belong the many speculations in the field of Christian Science, Theosophy and Anthroposophy. In "Seelsorge und Okkultismus" page 95 (92) some 20 forms of fortune-telling are enumerated. The technique of fortune-telling changes often, the spirit and the force that are behind it stay the same.

## VII. THE POSITION OF THE BIBLE

The Holy Scriptures are unanimous in their judgment, that is their rejection. At no period in the history of the people of Israel were fortune-tellers recognized. From ancient history to the time of Jesus and the writing of the New Testament books, fortune-telling in any form was rejected. Here are some evidences:

Leviticus 20, 6: And the soul that turneth after such as have familiar spirits (fortune-tellers) and after wizards (astrologers) I will ever set my face against that soul, and will cut him off from among the people.

Leviticus 20, 27: A man also or a woman that hath a familiar spirit, or that is a wizard, shall surely be put to death; they shall stone them with stones.

Deuteronomy 18, 10—12: There shall not be found among you any that useth divination, or an observer of times, or an enchanter, or a witch, or a charmer, or a consulter with familiar spirits, or a wizard, or a necromancer. For all that do these things are an abomination unto the Lord.

What was valid in the time of Moses continued to be valid also in the time of the kings and prophets.

I Chronicles 10, 13: So Saul died for his transgressions for asking counsel of one that had a familiar spirit to inquire of it.

Zachariah 10, 2: The diviners have seen a lie and have told false dreams.

Other passages are I Samuel 28, 6—21; Isaiah 8, 19; 44, 25; Ezekiel 21, 26; Micah 3, 6—7; Jeremiah 29, 8. The New Testament passage in Acts 16, 16—18 has already been discussed.

We want to keep in mind at this point, that fortune-telling in its scientific as well as in its primitive form stands under the judgment of God. God has given them up. That is the final reason why there are so many serious damages to body and soul with the many forms of fortune-telling. The effects shall be briefly recapitulated. It shall be explicitly pointed out that the compilation of effects represents only frequency appearances and not simple causality. Fortune-telling infected and occultly subjected people show with great frequency:

Regarding religion: The atheistic type shows resistance against all divine things, callousness, scepticism, calumnious disposition, inability to believe and pray. The 'pious' type shows self-righteousness,

61

spiritual pride, phariseeism, hypocrisy, insensitivity against the working of the Holy Spirit.

Regarding character: Abnormal passions are seen, tendency to addictions, instability (nicotine, alcohol, sexual vices) violent displays of temper, stinginess, gossiping disposition, egotism, cursing etc.

Regarding the medical point of view: In fortune-telling subjected families one finds remarkably many cases of nervous disturbances, psychopathic and hysteric symptoms, St. Vitus dance, symptoms of paralysis, epilepsy, freaks, deaf-mutes, mediumistic psychoses, tendency to emotional and mental illnesses etc.

To prevent quite primitive misunderstandings it must be pointed out that the concepts of fortune-telling and prophecy must not be confused. Prophecy comes from above, fortune-telling comes from below. Prophecy follows the inspiration of the Holy Spirit, fortune-telling is demonic, satanic inspiration. The woman fortune-teller in Philippi had a spirit from below. The prophet Agabus in Acts 21, 10 was directed by the Holy Spirit. We have to make an absolutely clear distinction between these two concepts.

## VIII. THE DELIVERANCE

There is a deliverance from the ban and the effects of fortune-telling. The Apostle Paul's meeting with the fortune-teller woman in Philippi led to a complete and immediate liberation of the woman. The Name of Jesus commanded these dark, demonic spirits. Jesus' victory at the cross of Golgotha is the sign that the power of darkness and hell is broken. Treatment of fortune-telling subjected people is therefore not first of all a problem for the psychiatrist, who is qualified only for purely medical concerns, but is a concern of the Christian counselor. Basically, deliverance is only possible through Jesus Christ. Therefore the person who is oppressed by fortune-telling troubles must come to Christ. At this time a general confession is indispensable. Confession in the Bible is a voluntary act. Protestant Christians reject every force. Yet in counseling I found not one occultly subjected person who could be liberated without the help of a confession.

In this paragraph Christian counseling methods, that were given already in other publications will not be repeated here. They are to be found in the book "Belastung und Befreiung" (Occult Subjection and Deliverance) and on the last 50 pages of "Seelsorge und Okkultismus" and of this book. Some deliverance examples shall be given here just for encouragement.

E 42　A girl from a Christian family worked in a big factory. In her department was a woman who layed cards for all the girls of the company. The Christian girl hesitated a long time to have cards layed for herself because from her childhood her mother had warned her of it. Finally her curiosity won. She went to see the card laying woman. The cards were shuffled and laid out on the table. Suddenly the card laying woman said abruptly to the girl: "I cannot lay cards for you."

E 43  A young woman was being treated magically for an organic disease. The lay medical practitioner used the pendulum to determine the medicines. One day this quack told her that in a few years she would be paralyzed. After a few years the woman actually developed symptoms of paralysis on the right side of her body. The arm and part of the leg became insensitive and immovable. At the same time she could no longer pray and read the Bible. A tremendous fear took hold of her. After a general confession I prayed with this woman under laying on of hands according to James 5,14. From this time on the paralysis was gone.

E 44  A woman went to a fortune-teller. She also repeatedly consulted a pendulum practitioner. From that time on she experienced strange spook phenomena in her house. She heard scratching and knocking noises and observed shadowy spooks. She was frightened by these experiences. She sought Christian counseling help and was shown the way to Christ. After she turned to Christ these spook phenomena in her house stopped.

These three examples show the power of faith in Christ. The girl from the believing family was surrounded by the prayers of her relatives. One experiences these things quite often, that people, for whom many are praying, are protected in the moment of danger. The magic power of the occult worker was suddenly paralyzed. The second example again shows the suggestive power of fortune-telling. In turning to Christ this woman was delivered from the suggestive spell. In the third example it is not evident whether the woman actually had authentic, objective spook experiences, or if it was only an illness (hallucination). In any case in turning to Christ she was freed of these strange disturbances. — The two following examples of deliverance are about the two strongest pendulum practitioners which I ever met.

E 45　A doctor discovered that he had the ability to use the pendulum. For eight days he conducted experiments. When a new patient entered the consulting-room he first offered him a chair. Then he went into an adjoining room and used the pendulum over the alphabet to find out the patient's first name, family name and disease. The result always proved to be in exact accordance with the examination that followed. These successes encouraged the doctor to conduct further experiments. When a nurse called from the branch office and reported new patients he used the same method. With the help of the pendulum and the alphabet he found out names, diseases and ages of the still unknown patients. The result always proved to be correct. These surprising successes encouraged him to increasingly difficult experiments. For instance if he wanted to know the time of departure or arrival of a train, the pendulum obligingly gave him the desired information. He could also with the help of the pendulum state names, ages, family relationships and other things of photos or group pictures of people. All fortune-telling and clairvoyant chances opened up to this pendulum practitioner.

During these experiments the doctor observed on himself psychic changes. He lost control of himself sexually also towards alcohol and nicotine. He often had fits of temper and did not know himself. Already after eight days of experimenting with the pendulum he had the feeling and fear of going insane. He stopped using the pendulum and in his inner confusion tried to find the way to Christ. He was given complete deliverance from the powers of the pendulum. Today this doctor is of the opinion that pendulum reaction depends on demonic forces, because he experienced the characteristic effects not only in his psychic but also in his religious life.

E 46   During a conference of evangelists in Switzerland I met an evangelist whose life story is a triumph of the grace of God. As a young man, after being cheated by his bride, he turned to fortune-tellers. Since all statements of the fortune-teller fulfilled themselves he became curious to learn the art for himself. He started using the pendulum and in this way he examined foods. Soon he turned to more profitable experiments. He used the pendulum to find out prices of the competitor, and he was successful. When afterwards he saw a price list of the competing firms, they agreed with his results. During the night he influenced his clients with a magic mirror and thereby forced their orders. Finally he also changed to healings of the sick. His diagnoses were accurate and he found the suitable medicines. Through magic charming he could also heal toothaches, stop bleeding, cure rheumatism, conduct treatments at distance and many more such things. When a lost object was to be located the pendulum always gave advice. Briefly two examples.

One day a transport plane crashed in the mountains. After an unsuccessful search the government offered a prize. He took the atlas and pendulum and determined the site of the crash to be at the foot of Piz Duan. He reported his findings. His information was not accepted, yet later the wreckage of the plane was found at the designated place. Once a skier was sought in Wallis. With the help of the pendulum and the map he quickly found the lost man. The high points of these pendulum experiments were his predictions. When in 1938 Germany acquired the Sudetic mountains, he asked the pendulum, if and when there would be war. The pendulum reacted over September 1939. This prediction did come true. As many pendulum practitioners he also thought to have received this ability as a gift from God. Furthermore he held this pendulum practice for a new science.

One day a Christian booklet was given to him. His eyes glanced over the passage Deut. 18, 10—12: "For all that do these things are an abomination unto the Lord." As if struck by lightning this word hit him. A great inward battle began. He threw away his pendulum literature and his books of magic and fought for liberation. Only now he realized whom he had served. In a booklet he wrote: "The devil, who through my activities had a claim to my soul, beat and tormented me incessantly." It came to a complete inner bankruptcy. Many months he fought and battled to be delivered. A prayer group started interceding for him. For 15 months it was an up-and-down battle. Hours of joy and faith changed with hours of depression. He still was not delivered from his magic, because he did not give up everything in this regard. He still held the pendulum practice for a science. Finally it was given to him to break with the pendulum also. All at once the pressure was lifted and a great peace entered his life. He had assurance that all of his sins were forgiven. Jesus Christ became the centre of his life. Since then he serves his Lord faithfully. During one of my evangelizations in Zurich he gave the closing message: From magician to evangelist. — If the Son therefore shall make you free ye shall be free indeed.

All these reports shall be ended with an example that shows the blessing of informative literature.

E 47  A young man of Christian background

learned to use the pendulum. He thought it to be a new science. He got engaged to a believing girl, who called his attention to the danger of the pendulum practice. She gave him Modersohn's book: "Under the Spell of the Devil" (Im Banne des Teufels). He recognized what was behind the pendulum practice and tried to get free. All of his efforts were unsuccessful. Spook phenomena appeared. His fiancé started a small prayer group which interceded for him. It was a year long battle before he was completely delivered through Christ.

# B. MAGIC

This chapter has been written out of the experience of Christian counseling as an information and a warning. Several thousand confessional talks show in a pathetic way how modern man cleaves to the old customs and magic practices in spite of the high standard of scientific knowledge. If these magic occurrences would only be harmless superstitions, a warning would not be very urgently needed. But as it is many people are being ruined psychically through magic. A recently held evangelization showed this need in a drastic way. A minister declared in the church council: "If during these informative lectures 49 out of 50 members of the congregation should be converted and one should be confused, then I would refuse this evangelization." In spite of this objection following the unanimous approval by the church elders, the evangelization was held. During that respective week over a hundred people came for Christian counseling. The sessions revealed that the community was disturbed by many occultly working quacks and nature healers. Many people were being magically treated and burdened by them daily. In the counseling sessions I heard the continous reproach by the psychically ill people: "Why does not the pulpit enlighten us about these forms of magic and sorcery?" With this we have the opinion from two sides, the local minister's and the congregation's.

Then we can turn around the above objection and ask: "Is it right, that 49 people are led astray because of lack of information and are brought under serious subjections by these magicians, so that one person may be protected from the possible harm of this information?" If we want to prevent harm in this way, then all propaganda for the prevention of addiction and communicable diseases would have to be stopped. Anyway our near sighted reflections whether or not we must inform are unimportant. The Bible gives us a watchman office. The prophet Ezekiel (3, 17—21) received the commission from God to warn the wicked. As members of the body of Jesus we cannot avoid this commission.

This watchman office is a difficult but hopeful service. What is to be said about the forces and powers of darkness comes from the victory of Jesus. The devil and his henchmen are indeed a terrible reality, but they are overcome and made powerless through Christ on the cross. He who comes to Jesus stands on victorious ground. All power in heaven and on earth is given unto Christ. Therefore we are not afraid. He who reads this writing now shall do so, looking unto Jesus, under whose strong hand we place ourselves.


## I. CONCEPT OF MAGIC

What do we understand under magic? The answer to such a question always depends upon the point of view of the critic. The psychologist, medical man, student of folklore, philosopher, believing occultist, liberal (de-mythologizing) theologian and the believing follower of Jesus — they all will have a different point of view about magic. The opinions here become sharply divided from the obtuse humbug theory to an addiction. Out of the experience of Christian counseling I want to formulate it this way: Magic is the disputed art or at least the attempt to know and rule the spirit world, human, animal and plant world as well as dead matter in an extrasensory way with the help of secret means and ceremonies. Let us briefly explain the different assertions of this definition.

1. The existence and ethical character of magic is hotly disputed. Psychiatry sees in the magical complex only the symptom of a mental illness. Psychology sees in the magically subjected person only the result of a wrong development, a superstitious maladjustment and wrong idea of life. Liberal theology also in its most modern form sees in magic time-bound customs and ideas.

No less hotly contested is the ethical character of magic. The one praises it as a gift of God, the other sees in it neutral forces of nature which can be used positively or negatively. Again others, especially the Christian counselors know about the demonic character of magic.

Why is it so difficult to judge magical occurrences? The above definition gives the answer. Magic

actions happen in an extrasensory way. Our five
senses only encompass a small area. This is the case
not only in the physical but also in the spiritual
realm. In physics man likes to admit it because
science furnishes the proof of these ultra-realms.
In the spiritual realm a mathematical demonstration is not possible therefore the nearsighted rationalists simply deny the existence of the divine and
the demonic.

2. Let us point out the extrasensory ways of
which the definition speaks. Here are a few examples.

E 48   The two Seiler brothers in Ottenheim, Baden, have a lay medical practice. In his office one
of the brothers puts himself into a trance. In this
condition he can recognize all diseases of the waiting patients. Afterwards he can give a correct diagnosis for all patients.

E 49   In Alsace a Catholic clergyman works as a
magic healer. He has the nickname: Pater Slipper.
The people desiring help must send him one of
their slippers. He concentrates on this slipper and
then can make a right diagnosis.

E 50   During counseling sessions in Austria I
happened to come across a so-called urin taster.
The patients' sent-in urin is not examined medically
regarding albumen, sugar, hamoglobin and other
admixtures, but serves as a psychometrical means
of contact for a clairvoyance diagnosis. Such urin

tasters are also known in Switzerland, France, Germany and other European countries.

The strange thing is that with such curious methods the diagnosis is often correct. These magic healing methods use mediumistic, extrasensory forces.

3. In the definition different objects of magic are named. In spiritism communication with the spirit world and its domination is being sought. Other objects of magic are people, animals, plants and dead matter. The black magician tries in a magic way to subjugate and dominate the enemy. There will be examples to this later on. Others also try to influence the animal and plant world. Here are some examples.

E 51   A milker engaged in black magic for many years. His specialty was to steal milk from the neighboring farmers. He tied a towel to his door handle, murmured his magic words and milked out of the towel. — I received such examples in Christian counseling. I could not examine them personally.

E 52   A missionary told me that several times when she tried to visit a magician wild animals approached her. She immediately felt that demonic powers were at work. When she commanded the animals in the Name of Jesus, they withdrew. Afterwards she heard that the magician had boasted, that he would send out wild animals to tear the approaching foreigner to pieces.

E 53   A young man, who the doctor described as schizophrenic, confessed to me during counseling, that he had the ability to kill small animals at distance, using no other means but his magic powers.

E 54   In Toggenburg (Canton St. Gallen) it was confessed to me several times in counseling sessions, that they (the confessors) could kill horses, cows and pigs with the help of black magic. In reply to my question how they had received this ability, they declared that they had subscribed themselves with their blood to the devil. One case of such mysterious animal killing was examined by some scientists but they could not uncover the cause.

E 55   A farmer, who had had several bad crops in a row received this advice from a magician. He should take three kernels of corn under his tongue while sowing. After he finished sowing, he should spit the three kernels on the field, say a magic charm and finish the act by calling the three highest names. In this way growth should be encouraged and the field protected from bad weather. As a matter of fact the farmer believed that the charming of this field had been benefical. But from this time on he did not want to have anything to do with the Word of God. In his stables there was also an enormous increase of accidents.

Not only the organic world and living creatures fall under magic's sphere of influence, but also the inorganic world of dead matter. Following are some examples.

E 56   For years three sister slept in one room. From time to time stones fell from the ceiling in this closed room. After the oldest sister became engaged and left the house, the rain of stones stopped. This occurrence was told to me by one of the three sisters. Such magic rains of stones are no rare occurrences. I have heard about it from eye witnesses.

E 57   For many years a man engaged in black magic. One of his special experiments, which he showed repeatedly was to push a knife into the ground. He murmured some magic words. Each time a pailful of blood came out at the point where the knife had struck. The sister of this black magician was also an expert in the field of black magic. It is the question whether this occurrence was only a skilful trick or a genuine magical occurrence. This example reminds us strongly of a fakir trick. Nevertheless similar incidents were reported to me in counseling talks.

In the sphere of magic the most absurd things happen. If everything existed only in the imagination and in superstition without any real background then this field would be already an abyss of human aberration and need, demanding enlightenment and counseling help. — Further questions pertaining to the definition will be discussed in the later paragraphs.

## II. ORIGIN, AIM AND DEVELOPMENT
## OF MAGIC

1. At the threshhold of human history stands the command of God: Replenish the earth and subdue it. (Gen. 1, 28). The task and right of man was the peaceful conquest of the earth's powers in agreement with the will of God. In opposition to this command, Satan, the great master of confusion, made the arch-temptation: Ye shall be as gods, knowing good and evil. (Gen. 3, 5). The antithesis of the command of God is magic, hunger for knowledge and desire for power in opposition to the will of God. With this young mankind found itself at the crossroads.

The points are shifted: voluntary subordination under the will of God, or compulsion for knowledge and greed for power in rebellion against divine rules and barriers. Today these points are still shifted. Either we let ourselves be fit into the divine pattern of the way of salvation, or we carry on a rebellion and try to rule the powers and beings of creation in a monstrous rivalry with God. Therefore magic is arch-rebellion from the beginning until today. It is the climax of man's revolt against God. All talk about harmless forces of nature and neutral application is an outrage in face of this Biblical fact.

Formally seen parapsychology (science of extra-sensory appearances) still knows something of the double character of magic. There one differentiates between Psi-Gamma phenomena (gignoskein — perceive) and Psi-Kappa phenomena (kinein-move). Here we have again the two basic elements of magic, knowledge and power through extrasensory ways.

2. Through many counseling talks I could recognize four different ways of origination of magical powers: heredity, subscriptions to the devil, occult experiments and occult transference.

a) The examination of many confessional reports proves that magical abilities are passed on in hereditary succession. Often mediumistic powers can be traced through four generations of one family. On the one hand the genes carry this dark ability, on the other hand these powers are carried on through succession. One understands under this the custom of the dying father bestowing upon his oldest son or daughter his magical abilities in order for him to die peacefully. Often tragedies occur in the death-chamber when the children do not want to have these abilities. The dying person can lament for weeks: "Take it away from me that I can find rest." Sometimes distant relatives or outsiders also are ready to take over the magical abilities. What role pity or curiosity or lust for power plays in this is different in each case. Sometimes the death of such magicians drags on over a period of weeks till the 'succession of office' has been settled. There is not only an apostolic but a diabolic succession.

b) A further form of origination of magical powers is devils' subscription. Perhaps one can see in this the counterpart to baptism. In everything magic is the demonic parallel to Biblical occurrences. Devil subscriptions are the most terrible cases for the Christian counselor.

E 58  In Paris, France, there is an occult church with the name: "We serve the prince of this world." This church has sister congregations in Basel, Berne and recently also in Rome. In order to become a member of this occult church one has to subscribe to the devil. That would be black magical baptism.

E 59  For years a man in Toggenburg, Switzerland had a flourishing practice as nature healer and charmer. He could even cure cases that had been given up by physicians. He healed the blind, lame, advanced cancer, tuberculosis of the lungs, leukemia, multiple sclerosis, scleroderma and other serious diseases. In a quiet hour this man cried out in distress: "I can help everybody. Only I cannot be helped in all eternity." In his youth this magic healer had made a devils' subscription. Since that time he possessed this uncanny healing ability.

c) Magical powers can also originate through occult experiments.

E 60  A Swiss factory worker became tired of his job. He often heard that occult healing practitioners and mesmerizers made a lot of money. So he bought himself magic literature from an occult publisher. He learned the magic charms, underwent devils' ceremonies and began healing experiments. His magic healing ability developed rapidly and finally his income surpassed many times his former wages.

The following example unites all three aspects: heredity, subscription and occult experiments.

E 61  A young woman told me the story of her ancestors. Her great-grandmother had subscribed herself to the devil with her blood. She practiced black magic and healed sick people and animals. On her deathbed she suffered terrible agonies, as it is usual with these magic conjurers. The daughter, who was the grandmother of the young woman, took over the magic powers from the dying woman. She also took over her magic literature. After her painful death the great-grandmother's apparition was seen by her relatives. The grandmother then continued the magical practice. She charmed diseases during nights of the full moon.

She was also a pendulum practitioner and was successful in stopping bleedings. When the grandmother began to read the Bible she had serious troubles. As she grew older she saw black figures in her room. She also had a very difficult death. Her apparition was also seen after her death. Then the mother of the young woman took over the magical literature and practice. She also became a well-known healer. Her fate was the same as her predecessors'. Now the fourth member of this terrible family tree was this young woman. When she had been a small child her own mother had spoken charms over her. Shortly after this charming she had become clairvoyant and had seen black figures in the house. Her brother and sister suffered from depressions. She herself had serious psychic and nervous disturbances which led her to seek Christian counseling help.

d) The fourth form of origination of magical powers is occult transference.

E 62    A young man told me in a counseling session that three black magicians had put their hands on his head and had murmured magic charms. Afterwards he had possessed magic faculties which astonished even the family physician. The doctor tested him and had to acknowledge his magic healings. This magical laying on of hands would again be the counterpart to the Biblical laying on of hands.

E 63    A young man watched a pendulum practitioner who was searching for water with the pendulum. The pendulum practitioner suggested that he try it once. But the pendulum did not react in his hand. Then the pendulum practitioner held the hand of the young man. Suddenly the pendulum reacted in the hand of the young man also. When afterwards he repeated this act without the help of the pendulum practitioner, he was successful again. Even after a few days he still had this ability. Since this contact with the pendulum practitioner the young man possesses the ability to search for water with the pendulum or divining rod. But something has been changed in his life of faith.

Before that time he had been faithful in prayer and reading of the Bible. After the transference of the pendulum ability his love for the Word of God and prayer declined.

## III. FORMS OF MAGIC

Several preliminary steps of suggestion point to magic.

1. First criminal hypnosis will be discussed.

E 64   A girl reported in a counseling session that the doctor whom she had consulted, had hypnotized her. While being hypnotized he had attacked her in the consulting room. He had repeated this also with her girl friend. Afterwards it was known that he had also done this with other girls. When these stories leaked out, the doctor left town and settled elsewhere. Then the girl told, that after this incident she could not read the Word of God for years. She felt a strong resistance against all divine things and always had dirty thoughts while praying.

E 65   A hospital physician abused women and girls under hypnosis. Once the head nurse caught him in the act. To cover up his scandalous acts, he questioned the patients, while writing down their history, about their marital or premarital relations. Then he wrote the answers into the history. Thus he tried to protect himself if any incident should be charged against him. A girl with a good reputation, who was engaged to a Christian young man, became pregnant in this hospital. Following this her fiancé left her. According to her confessional statements, she never before in her life had had marital relations. She had been attacked by this doctor under hypnosis. Finally the head nurse and the ward nurse reported this doctor. The result was that the two nurses were dismissed by the medical superintendent. The doctor himself stayed. Other nurses, who had charges against this doctor were silent, because of the dismissal of the two nurses. This report was given to me by a nurse who had been a witness to these shady stories. When after a few years it was no longer safe for the doctor to stay he went abroad.

Scientific advocates of hypnosis believe that man cannot be forced to do anything while under hypnosis which he would not do while being awake. They are of the opinion that crimes are not possible under hypnosis. It should be noted first that not all scientific experts share this opinion. Besides in my counseling work I have known of many cases where crimes happened under hypnosis. From the Biblical point of view it is understandable that a still untouched girl can be abused under hypnosis. Jesus says: "Out of the heart of man come evil thoughts." Bad things slumber even in the most moral people. Consciousness, which is formed by character disposition, education and religious attitude rules and holds down all conative things. Under hypnosis this regulator has been eliminated. Conative impulses can rise up unhindered from the subconscious and can be exploited by unscrupulous people without inhibitions. Furthermore these scientific experts do not take into account the fact that there is a magical hypnosis beside normal hypnosis which reaches much further in its effectiveness than normal hypnosis. Magic hypnosis can often be recognized by the fact that afterwards the patient can no longer believe or pray. Some examples of magic hypnosis shall follow.

E 66   A Christian girl went to a psychiatrist. The psychiatrist did not only use normal hypnosis but mainly magic hypnosis. Occasionally I happened to come across such doctors in areas where much magic is being practiced. In reply to a question by the believing girl during one session, the doctor answered that he had not received this gift from God. He also confessed to the questioner that he had wanted to conduct a suggestive experiment on her. After this treatment the girl could no longer believe or pray. She had doubts and other serious difficulties in believing.

The following is a very unusual example

E 67   In his spare time a minister occupied himself with magic. He experimented in different fields. He learned how to lay cards, how to use the pendulum, also magic charming and magic hypnosis. Because he had no suitable people for his experiments he carried them out on his wife. As his magical abilities increased so the ministers' and his wife's dislike for the Word of God and prayer increased. Dislike grew into strong resistance. In connection with these magical experiments psychic disturbances also developed. The minister's wife developed serious anxiety hysteria. She always had to lock the room in which she happened to be.

E 68   A businessman has the strange ability to influence his customers hypnotically or magically so that they consent to all of his offers. In this way his yearly earnings total about 70 000 DM. He completely rejects all divine things.

E 69   Before a treatment a woman had a masseur hypnotize her. Before the hypnotical treatment she read the Bible, prayed and attended church services. Afterwards when she tried to pray she felt a compulsion to blaspheme the name of God and to curse. She rejected all divine things. The effects of this treatment show that the masseur had worked with magic hypnosis.

Our medical men in general do not understand anything about magically based hypnosis because this form belongs to occult practices. While normal hypnosis, practiced by medical men, can be harmless, the connection of hypnosis with magic is always dangerous and subjects the patient.

2. A further preliminary form of magic is mental suggestion. Under this one understands a transference at distance of mental or emotional forces.

E 70   A young psychologist wanted to qualify

himself for lecturing at universities. His specialty was hypnosis, yet not normal hypnosis but mental suggestion at distance. He searched for a sensitive subject for his experiments. He found one in the secretary of his boss who was neurasthenic and easily influenced. Without asking he started to put her to sleep. He sat down at a distance of 10 feet in the same room or even in a neighboring room and concentrated on the girl. Suddenly the secretary's arms became lame. A tremendous tiredness came over her. She fought with all her strength against falling asleep. These experiments were continued over a period of time always with the girl resisting them. During this time of hypnotic experiments the girl gradually developed psychic disturbances. She consulted a psychiatrist. When he heard of these suggestive experiments he declared: "That is not good for you." But the psychiatrist knew about the hypnotic experiments of the young psychologist. These experiments had been carried on over a long period of time. Since that time the girl was not able to work full time and repeatedly felt strange paralytic symptoms.

E 71   A Catholic woman often went to a priest for confession. Finally she became psychically and suggestively dependent on him. Every time he said mass she fell to the ground and hurt herself. She always injured her face. The attacks happened even if she was 20 mi. away from the priest and did not know when he said mass. This strange dependence became an unbearable burden to this woman. In her distress she started to pray seriously. She went to a Protestant clergyman for counseling. By faith she found the way to a personal relationship to Christ. From this moment on the strange attacks ceased. The woman then left the Catholic church.

E 72   For several years a worker occupied himself with black magic. He was mostly interested in magic practices through which he could influence other people. He also belonged to a magic circle which conducted strange experiments. In his spare-time he personally tried out these experiments. His first victim was a sensitive girl which he brought under his power to such an extent that she made all financial and sexual sacrifices. After this successful beginning as a black magician he searched for other victims. His experiments were successful. Finally he found a girl who regularly turned her monthly paycheck over to him. For this reason he took the girl into his house. She lived with him for some time until her parents reported the man to the police.

3. The third preliminary form of magic is magically based mesmerism. Magnetism as well as hypnosis and suggestion can be magically intensified. In E 69 a similar example was given.

First an example from Dr. Trampler. This lawyer is a student of Groening but later came to a parting of the ways with his teacher. Dr. Trampler has revealed his healing methods in a book: 'Gesundung durch den Geist' (Healing through the spirit). Women are his most fanatical followers. Through several examples from Christian counseling I could observe that the healing powers that Trampler makes use of are not beneficial to the patients but put them under subjection. Two examples shall show this.

E 73   A woman visited Dr. Trampler in Munich. He successfully treated her against her backaches. In his office she had to raise her ten fingers as antenna for cosmic powers. After she returned home she had been indeed healed organically but from that day on she had spiritual difficulties instead. She could no longer pray and felt that there was an impenetrable wall between her and God.

E 74   A Christian woman, who came to me for counseling, visited Dr. Trampler in ignorance. She sat in his office praying. One patient after the other was treated. Finally Dr. Trampler stood in front of her. Since she felt a strange fear, she prayed more earnestly. Then Dr. Trampler declared: "I cannot do anything for you."

Since these healers often camouflage and garnish their activities with religious words, the terrible nature of their powers is often not recognized. In Baden I became acquainted with a lay medical practitioner, who had experienced a clear conversion to Christ. In reply to my question regarding his healing ability he answered: "Natural healing magnetism is enough for about two patients daily.

Then the power is used up and has to be newly gathered or charged. He who treats more than two patients a day accomplishes nothing — or he has his plug box below." By this he meant that these quacks would practice magic additionally. One more example for this often practiced, confusing camouflage.

E 75　A friend of mine, a Christian teacher, was being treated by a mesmerizer who was supposed to be a Christian. He attended church services. To be sure the teacher asked the mesmerizer: "You do not use demonic forces, do you?" The quack replied: "But demonic powers are good. The demons do help us." Thereupon the teacher decided not to take the treatment.

4. After the different preliminary forms the main forms of magic must be shown. Prof. Diepgen differentiates in his book: "Culture and Medicine" between three forms of magic: black magic with the help of demonic powers, white magic allegedly with divine help, and neutral magic, allegedly an application of neutral forces of nature. Diepgens differentiations are correct but not the definitions. Concerning point two and three Christian counseling gives a completely different picture.

a) First a few examples of black magic.

E 76　A minister told me that his whole congregation was infected with occult things. As an example he told of a magic healing of a 20 year old girl. Because of an attack of polio the girl had a shortened leg. She had been in the hospital for a long time and then had been released as incurable. The girl and her mother were very depressed. Finally they sought help from a man who practiced black magic. This magician made them pay DM 500.— for the purchase of a mandrake root. This root, which resembled a human had to be nursed like an infant by the patient, according to the instructions of the magician. All activities like washing, bathing, feeding, putting to sleep, had to be carried out according to the rules of infant care. After this first phase of treatment the magician ordered he girl to pray psalms of vengeance, also to copy out such psalms, lay them under her pillow and sleep on them. During the third phase of treatment the girl had to put two knives under her pillow and stick two other knives into the wall at the head of the bed. In the course of this extremely strange therapy the girl experienced her shortened leg to become longer. After her leg had been healed the patient developed serious psychic disturbances. She went to her minister who was helpless when faced with this case. The girl could no longer pray. When she tried to fold her hands they were torn apart. When she tried to read the Bible she had blasphemous thoughts. The girl feared for her sanity so she finally handed over to the minister the mandrake root and an amulet which she had received from the magician. From this moment on she lived in great fear of revenge from this terrible man. The leg, which had been stretched to normal length during the magic treatment shortened itself again.

E 77 During an evangelization in Toggenburg a farmer came for counseling and told me the unhappy results of black magic charming. His boy had contracted polio. The doctor was called in too late and the boy remained paralyzed. Since the farmer under any condition wanted a healthy heir to take over the farm he tried everything possible. Finally he went to the notorious magician Hugentobler in Peterzell. He healed the boy with the help of black magic, so that his paralysis disappeared completely. For several years everything went well. When the son was 16 years of age the father found him in the stable with a cut carotid artery. This misfortune happened out of a blue sky. There was no quarrel in the family neither was a girl involved. On his fatally wounded son the father found an amulet from Hugentobler. He opened the leather pouch and pulled out a piece of paper with the inscription: 'This soul belongs to the devil.' That was the evidence that Hugentobler had used black magic in this case.

b) Even more widely spread than black magic is the so-called white magic. It is carried on in many Christian circles as pious activity without the participants being aware of its demonic character. In white magic the word of St. Paul is fulfilled in II Cor. 11, 14 that Satan himself is transformed into an angel of light. White magic is black magic under pious camouflage. Here are a few examples.

E 78　A missionary to the Jews of North Africa by the name of Samuels, reported a magic custom of the North African Jews. When in the Jewish families a child becomes sick the parents take a towel, tie a knot in it and say: "In the name of the God of Abraham, Isaac and Jacob, be released from your sickness." Then they open the knot, and the children get well from that time on through the magic charming. This is a counterpart to black magic.

E 79　A woman from Bukowina reported that her relatives use white magic healing charms in all sicknesses of humans and animals. To the charm they added the three highest names. After this charming the sickness disappeared. Although all of her ancestors were church people these different healing charms were passed on from generation to generation. The woman and her daughter suffer from nervous disturbances. That was her reason for seeking counseling help. A preacher prayed with her. Afterwards her disturbances improved. She also received assurance of salvation.

E 80　The owner of a farm hanged himself in his house. According to the popular belief of the villagers the suicide is supposed to haunt the place of his deed. Therefore the relatives were advised to sweep out the whole house in the three highest names. After this the suicide would not trouble the house. As a matter of fact the relatives followed this strange advice. But from this time on the farmer's wife was troubled with a strange unrest.

E 81   A fifteen year old girl had an eye disease. She spent quite some time in an eye clinic, but in spite of the medical treatment she did not get well. Since the help of the doctors had failed she availed herself of the help of the magic charmer. The man spoke charms over her according to the way of white magic. In his room was a Bible. From time to time he attended church services. Within 24 hours after the charming the girl's eye trouble disappeared. But from the time of the healing she felt a terrible unrest. She searched for Christ in prayer but could not find peace. When after this strange healing she visited her former eye specialist, he only shook his head in astonishment and asked her how this healing had occurred.

E 82   A woman had her two daughters charmed magically in their earliest youth. During this magic treatment the charmer used the Lord's prayer three times. As the children grew up the mother was repeatedly advised by astrologers, through card laying and palmistry. She also received the monthly magazine of an occult doctor. The oldest daughter was placed into a mental institution at the age of 27 and is considered incurable. The whole family strongly rejected all divine things. Now after their psychic distress reached a certain high point, they sought Christian counseling advice.

E 83   A Christian woman had several white magic recipes. Against scurvy of the mouth she ordered Easter water which had to be taken with the three highest names.

E 84   A seriouly ill woman laid in the hospital with shingles and leg ulcers. Her condition was so bad that the doctor ordered a private night nurse. One counted with the patient's death. The night nurse sat next to the bed of the dying woman. Repeatedly the patient whispered to the nurse: "Nurse, you can help me." The nurse was afraid that the woman wanted her to pray or say a word from the Bible, but the patient did not want a Biblical word. Anyway the nurse would not have been in a position to do that. She was full of fear in the presence of the sick woman and could not utter a prayer for herself. The woman constantly repeated the sentence: "Nurse you can help me" so she finally asked: "How should I help you then?" Suddenly the woman became quite animated and explained: "I will uncover my body, you must put your hand on the sick parts, make three crosses over it, name the trinity and say a short verse which I will tell you." The night nurse was even more scared. At that moment a doctor went through the hall and she asked him whether she should fulfil the wish of the patient. The doctor encouraged her and replied: "Go ahead and do it, nurse. Maybe it will help the patient. Besides there is no more hope humanly and medically speaking." The nurse then returned to the death room and immediately the sick woman urged her again to start with the charming process. The nurse made three crosses on the sick body of the patient, named the three highest names and murmured the charms that the woman told her. Then immediately the sick woman could rest. But the nurse felt a tremendous fear and unrest. During the next days all of the doctors were greatly astonished. The open leg ulcers closed up immediately, the whole disease symptoms disappeared completely within five days. The doctors could not explain this surprizing turn of events. The doctor who had advised the charming kept this incident to himself. It is now six years since that charming occurred but the nurse has not found her peace again. She can no longer pray. She turns in disgust from God's Word and all divine things. Her head is often dazed, she cannot concentrate properly and has psychic disturbances. This condition led her to me for counseling. She personally traces back her serious psychic disturbances to the terrible incident of charming. Without her knowledge she had helped the patient with white magic.

In all of these magic examples the Christian symbols and the number three play a role. Charming is done in the three highest names, in using three Lord's prayers or three Bible verses. Three crosses are made or three blessed candles are used. White magic is the cunning perversion of the Biblical prayer of faith under laying on of hands. That

95

is the reason why so many fall victim to this religious magic.

The differentiation between white magic and Biblical laying on of hands is often very difficult, even if the basic differences are known.

In the Biblical prayer of faith the praying person puts himself under the will of God. In white magic the help of God shall be forced. In the Biblical prayer there is an inner contact of the praying person with his God. In white magic the Christian elements are only being used as technical means of magic. The person who prays Biblically stands under the inspiration of the Holy Spirit, which helps his infirmities. The white magician stands under the inspiration from below. The person who prays Biblically is being strengthened in his faith after his prayer even if the prayed-for help was not granted by God in the desired form. The active and passive white magician is afterwards severely disturbed and paralyzed in his faith life, if he possesses one in the first place, even if the forced help came according to his wishes. Often it can be seen by the effects only, if the prayer was Biblical or magical. The boundaries can be fluid. Sometimes the critic must have the gift of discerning of spirits if he wants to find his way through the genuine and camouflaged occurrences. White magic does not need counseling for its procedure; Biblical laying on of hands only follows a previous, thorough counseling session. White magic procedures will be decidedly disturbed or made impossible by a person present who prays. The Biblical laying on of hands is supported and strengthened by other persons who pray. White magic and the Biblical laying on of hands are totally different, even if similar sounding words are being used.

c) A further form is the so-called neutral magic. Recently it has been used by doctors in the psychosomatic school. They believe they can employ neutral forces of nature that are neither positive nor negative for healing purposes. Several examples are before me which are highly equivocal.

E 85    A young minister, who had many warts on his hand, asked the chief of a psychosomatic advanced class: "Professor, how do I get rid of the warts?" The professor replied: "There is only one proven method, namely charming." The minister was instructed and the procedure of magic charming was a complete success. I was not told of eventual after effects. The man who was freed from his warts was silent about them.

E 86    A young psychiatrist asked the chief of a psychiatric clinic: "Professor, how do I get rid of my warts?" The professor gave the following advice: "Bind the warts with a black thread. Make as many knots in the thread as you have warts, then say a magic verse and lay the thread under a gutter. Then you are rid of the ugly things." At first the doctor thought it was a joke. Finally he was talked into trying it out. The experiment was successful above all expectations. The warts disappeared.

This professor's suggestion is not neutral magic. This strange recipe is written in the 6th and 7th Book of Moses, which contains only black and white magic charms. As yet this supposedly neutral magic could not prove its neutrality and harmlessness. Counseling reveals continous evidence that magic is devil's work whether it sails under black, white or neutral flag.

## IV. AREAS OF APPLIED MAGIC

The chapter concerning objects of magic has pointed out already that everything we human beings believe to exist in heaven and on earth and under the earth, falls under the firing range of magic. It is the program of the world-wide arch-rebellion of Satan, that God and Christ, angels and spirits, all living things on earth and matter should be attacked. It is simply impossible to describe the tremendous span of magic in this book. Only a few main areas can be pointed out.

1. Healing and Bringing on Sickness. Many examples of healing have already been given. Only one more shall follow.

E 87  A Catholic woman was seriously ill in a hospital. The sick woman called the nurse and asked of her the following favour. She told her that she had a daughter at home who had been possessed for years. Very rarely was her daughter conscious. Now because she was so seriously ill she had an apportunity to help her plagued daughter. Then she asked the nurse: "Please notify my relatives before I die. My possessed daughter will then be brought here. Then the two of us will change shirts. With this act I take the possession of my daughter to the grave. Through this my daughter will be freed." The nurse did not fulfil the wish of the dying woman.

The opposite of healing is bringing on sickness.

E 88   A young man wanted to evade military service. Therefore his father sent him to a magic charmer who should give him a disease. The experiment was successful. Afterwards the young man was unfit for military service.

E 89   A spiritistic medium confessed that she belonged to a circle which practiced not only communication with the dead but also black magic. Her specialty was bringing on sickness and death magic. She had already committed several murders which the police could not solve. She had also harassed a minister, who afterwards developed nervous disturbances and was unable to work for several months. This was the content of the confession. I could not prove these statements. I only know that during the time of the circle's magic experiments, this minister was sick for a longer period of time.

E 90　A girl from a strict Catholic family married
a Protestant man against the will of her parents.
The first born son of this marriage contracted polio.
The parents blamed their daughter with these
words: "This is the punishment for your marriage
to a Protestant." The Catholic parents then ordered
a magician to heal the son and to plague or bring on
a sickness on the mother instead. As a matter of fact
the son got well surprizingly fast, but the mother
became sick. The woman was taken to the hospital
with strange disturbances, symptoms of paralysis,
depression, terrible headaches etc. The doctors dif-
fered in their diagnosis. They made one special test
after another, spinal puncture, basic metabolism
test, electro-cardiogram etc. Finally they called in
a brain specialist. The examinations lasted several
weeks, but they found no cause. Finally the condition of the woman improved rapidly. She asked to
be released. The doctors agreed. The Catholic parents were greatly disturbed about this turn of
events, and immediately reported to the magician
that his persecution had become ineffective.

E 91　A black magician said to a girl, who was
courted by well-situated married man: "I'll break
this man's mind to such an extent that he will lose
his position." It was not very long before this man
experienced nervous disturbances. He complained
about knocking noises in and outside of his head,
about twitching and reduction of visual acuity and
power of concentration.

E 92   A girl accepted Christ during an evangelization. In her exuberance over her new-found joy, she tried to invite her neighbors also to the meetings and Bible classes. In her neighborhood lived a man who possessed an extensive literature of occult books and experimented with them. The joyful witness of this believing girl did not set right with this man. (The Gospel of Christ and magic are divided as heaven and hell.) The occultist threatened: "I'll make her crazy, that she'll no longer go to the meetings." Indeed after a few weeks this believing girl developed disturbances. She saw little flames of light in her room and other spook phenomena. In this condition she came to me for counseling.

2. L o v e   a n d   H a t e   M a g i c. Examples 90 to 92 can also be put under hate magic. A few examples of love magic shall follow.

E 92   Swiss cowherders who bring down the cattle from summer pasture in September, like to tie three little herbs into the rope of the lead cow. It shall not only serve as decoration but shall bring luck in love.

E 94   A girl had an affair with a married man. One day this man changed his place of residence. Before he moved he explained to his girl friend: "Though we are separated now I will continue to visit you. I will not drive back here but I will only meet you in dreams. You know what a man wants from a girl. I can take what I need anytime, you cannot prevent it. You will never be able to do anything against me for you have no evidence for it." At first the girl did not understand much of this strange explanation. A week after her friend had left she suddenly felt his presence during the night. The visits were repeated again and again till the strange meetings became terrible and disgusting to the girl. First she consulted a doctor. As was to be expected, the doctor explained these nightly psychic meetings as sexual hallucinations in the beginning stages of schizophrenia. The girl, who is mentally completely sound, does not accept the diagnosis of this doctor but believes that other factors are involved.

3. Persecution and Defence Magic belong to the most common forms of magic practices.

E 95 Two Bessarabic women who practiced magic for many years got into a fight. Both used their magic powers to persecute the other. One woman fell to the ground during this fight without any visible cause, showed symptoms of paralysis and could not get up again. She swore and cursed her opponent. When she was being lifted off the ground she screamed at the other woman: "You won't leave this house alive. I'll see to it." Three days later the threatened woman had a terrible headache and after eight days she was dead.

E 96 A child cried every night from 11 to 1 o'clock. The desperate mother was advised by a magician. She was told to put a knife, a fork and a pair of scissors under the child's pillow, then these annoyances would stop. Also the respective culprit should injure himself through this magic defence. The troubled mother followed this advice. When a day later the chamber maid wore a bandage, she was convinced that the chamber maid had been the cause of the nightly disturbance.

E 97 A farmer observed that the milk of one of his cows was bloody. He heated the bloody milk at night between 11 and 12 o'clock, stuck a sickle in and murmured a charm. The next day a neighbor woman had injuries in her face. He now supposed that this neighbor woman had bewitched his cow.

4. Casting and breaking spells is being practiced by some magicians as a sport, others use it to further their selfish interests.

E 98 A man in a Christian convalescent home had the ability to cast and break magic spells. He could stop people on the street so that they could not move from the spot. He could also ban children that they could not speak or take another step. This man was supposed to be a believing Christian.

E 99 In Switzerland an officially licensed mesmerizer treats his patients with white magic charms. He either uses the three highest names or three Lord's prayers. Because of these pious words he is believed to be a Christian by his patients. This mesmerizer possesses magic powers. When a patient does not pay right away he puts him under a spell. On his departure he can go as far as the station but cannot enter the train. The station personnel know about the magic powers of the mesmerizer from manifold observations and tell the patient laughingly: "First pay the mesmerizer, then you can come back and take the train."

E 100 For years a school teacher occupied himself with black magic. He not only provided himself with literature about it but made magic experiments. His objects of experiment were his school children. He called upon the children while at the same time he cast a spell. The called child could neither get up from his place nor talk. Only after he broke the spell was the child able to get up and answer. This method he also used as a punishment. After he had practiced for years on his school children he used his own wife and daughter as further objects of experiment. He ruled his family so completely that he could cast spells over them at will. Sometimes his wife and daughter could not speak a word for hours or even days. His wife was psychically destroyed and she died. The second wife ran out on him and never returned after his first banning experiment. Thereupon the father attacked his daughter sexually. The daughter was completely powerless in defending herself against the father. When the father turned to a third woman he cast a spell over his daughter. She suffered a permanent speech paralysis. Because the daughter stood in the way of the father and his many women he had her committed into a mental institution. The doctors were not able to overcome the speech paralysis. The girl's relatives, who know about the terrible home conditions, are forbidden by the father to visit the unfortunate girl in the institution.

5. Death Magic on animals and humans belongs to the darkest part of magic. I have before me several missionary reports on this subject. Only few people know that such things are also being practiced in Europe. Even if the effectiveness of death magic cannot be proved, the mere existence of such customs implies the low level of our culture.

E 101  A black magic expert specialized in magic persecution, death magic and stable magic. With the help of black magic he was able to kill a cow in four days. This report comes from the man's grandson.

E 102  For years a woman practiced black magic. She possessed very dangerous magic books, for instance the 6th and 7th Book of Moses, the Spring Book, the Spiritual Shield, and many other occult books. She experimented in the area of black magic persecution and death magic. She boasted: "I have done away with my husband and my daughter." She persecuted her enemies with diseases. She declared that she could cause excemas, diarrhoea, heart trouble, itching, stomach aches, swelling of the body and other things on her enemies. After she brought about the death of her whole family in this manner, according to her own words, she got the job of parish nurse through the help of a minister. Now as ever the woman still practices magic. She is

closed against all divine things. She calls Jesus a
S.O.B. and a good-for-nothing. On church holidays
she has terrible attacks where she falls into a rage
and blasphemes. In her good hours her conscience
bothers her and she declares: "My life is a mess.
I don't want to do what I am driven to do. But I
must do ist. The devil drives me. I can never find
rest."

E 103   A married man carried on adulterous relations with an older single girl. This girl has the
reputation of working with black magic. One day
the man got tired of this illicit affair. He told the
girl that he would break off with her. She was very
upset and threatened him: "You have a wife and
two children. They will have to suffer for this."
The man was not intimidated by this and stuck to
his decision. Two days after the separation his son
became ill, was taken to the hospital and died. It
was a strange disease which could not be diagnosed
by the physicians. A few days later his wife and
daughter also became sick. The man was frightened
and thought of the threats of the magic charmer
who had been his girl friend. He rushed to her and
implored her earnestly not to use black magic
against him. She softened and declared: "Well, I'll
drop it then." Afterwards the wife and daughter
recovered quickly.

E 104   During an evangelization a man came for
Christian counseling and reported the following
case from his village. His neighbor's new saw had

been stolen. The theft took place in broad daylight and had been observed. The neighbor was immediately notified about the act and the thief's name was also reported to him. The saw's owner was not satisfied with a report to the police. He went to a man who carried on persecution experiments with the help of black magic. The victim of the theft made his request known and paid the magic expert a large fee. This occultist promised immediate help and declared: "The thief must die." Then the farmer drove back to the village. Three hours after the consultation with the occultist the thief had a fatal heart attack.

## V. THE MAGIC RITES

Magic in all its forms and customs has the character of a devil's religion. In everything it mimics the Biblical world of faith.

1. Magic liturgy is the counterpart of the Biblical worship service and forms of worship. A magic action usually is composed of four elements: Invocation, charm, symbolic action, use of a fetish. The invocation is to the trinity or to Satan. It decides whether black or white magic shall be used. The invocation is the counterpart to our mode of adress: Our Father our our Lord Jesus Christ. The charms then bring the magic powers into action. The magic charm is the counterpart to the Biblical Word or to

the Biblical prayer. The symbolic action under-
scores the charm. The symbolic action mimics the
Biblical symbolic action, as for instance the laying
on of hands or forms of prayers. The use of a fetish,
which is a magically charged object corresponds
perhaps to the use of water or bread and wine in
the Christian realm.

E 105  A farmer's son suffered repeatedly from
severe pain on his knee. According to the advice
of a charmer, he carried out the following magic
treatment. During the time of the waning moon he
went out into the field at night. He invoked the
trinity, said a magic charm, anointed his knee with
oil and threw kisses to the moon. Afterwards the
pains were gone.

This example contains the following facts: Invocation of the trinity decides the form of magic, in
this case white magic. The magic charm takes the
place of prayer. Anointing with oil is a symbolic
action. The moon is being used as a fetish. As he is
waning, so the pain should wane.

2. M a g i c  s y m b o l i s m is supposed to support
the magic charm in its effectiveness. At the same
time magic transference takes place. Because of
lack of space the character of occult transference
cannot be discussed here. Examples shall show the
problem.

E 106  Professor Frobenius, the well-known spe-
leologist (cave researcher) reported in a lecture that
some of the cave drawings of stone-age man could

be understood as hunting magic. Some of the animals are drawn with wounds. The observation would be in accordance with the hunting magic of the primitive people of Africa. An African traveller told that native tribes sometimes make use of hunting magic and actually are successful. They draw animals and shoot at the picture while saying magic charms. The same day animals are found during the hunt with the same wounds as those in the drawings. This primitive hunting magic corresponds also to observations in Germany. If human or animal phantoms are injured then the medium is thereby injured in like manner.

E 107   In the area of magic charming the following recipe is given against toothaches. A new nail must be pushed into the gums three times. Then the nail must be buried in the cellar facing East while saying a magic charm.

E 108   A school child had a swelling on the arm and a charm was spoken over her. A chicken egg was buried and a stone put on top of it while saying a charm. In the measure as the egg disintegrated in the soil, the swelling went down. Magic symbolism was successful.

Magic symbolism is usally being supported through a fetish. Under fetish one understands a magically charged object. The fetish shall be the carrier of power. Mainly absurd things are being used as fetish, for instance human bones, bats, urin, excrement, pubic hair, finger nails, coffin wood and many other things. Any object that has been magically charmed and charged can become a fetish. An example.

E 109  A preachers' wife received a salve from a woman church member, which had been produced by a magic charmer while speaking magic charms. The salve helped rapidly. It did not work as a medicine but as a fetish, as a power charged object. After this treatment the preacher's wife broke her arm. Her daughter, who had made good progress in the life of faith before this could no longer believe or pray.

E 110  During an evangelization in Switzerland I was told in counseling that a Catholic monastery gives out little amulets (fetishes) to the people against diseases and epidemics. They consist of small bags. A curious person cut one of those bags open. Inside were toe nails and egg shells. This report sounds very improbable, but I am sad to say that I often observed that some monasteries practice magic.

3. The significance of the m a g i c  w o r d is very much debated. A well-known representative of charming, Traugott Egloff in Zurich speaks of the directness of the word and explains, the word is a power in itself which produces miracles. We believe, if the charmer uses Bible words, he severs them from God, isolates them and idolizes the spoken word. He sets up the creature against the Creator. This isolation of the word leads to mechanical usage

and with it to depletion. In this connection Prof. Bender says: "The mechanistic is the real essence of magic and diabolism."

The word which is isolated and severed from God cannot exist independently. Foreign contents flood in. What has been severed and fallen off from God falls prey to the demons. Therefore the mechanical and magic use of Bible words is sorcery and of the demons. The Word of God, given for the salvation of man, turns into a magical technique, burdening and harming man.

We oppose the belief that the word is a power in itself which the charmer represents for it is only a neutral instrument. It can be used for good and evil. It depends upon the inspiration that stands behind the word, whether it comes from above or from below. The disciple of Jesus uses the word as authorized by God. The magician, the charmer uses the word as a demonized instrument of magic.

E 111 A minister told me about a strange death in his congregation. A man, who had the reputation of being a magician was dying. For fourteen days the dying man groaned: "Take the word from me, take the word from me, that I can find rest." The relatives went to the minister for advice. He warned them from fulfilling the request of the dying man. After terrible agonies the magician died. The minister said that the man looked black as coal in the coffin. — Many magicians find rest only after somebody has taken the magic charm from them and with it the responsibility of carrying on the charming practice.

4. The Magic Ritual.

There are magic books which have the same importance for the magician as the Bible has for the Christian. Occult literature exists in great numbers. The most widely distributed in our time is the 6th and 7th Book of Moses. It is a sad thing that a publishing firm in Braunschweig has published new editions of this book. The book has nothing to do with Moses. The name is only a cover-up. The miracle of the staff of Moses was interpreted by magicians as magic. Therefore they thought they could elevate Moses as their patron saint. The sixth Book shows how man can enter into relationships with the devil. The seventh Book gives instructions as to how man can achieve dominion through magic over all powers in earth, heaven and hell. They are magic books which have already caused untold harm in our country. People who read this book are unfortunates; houses where this book is kept are houses of misfortune. There are a great number of examples, but due to lack of space they cannot be used here. E 113 and 115 belong in this category.

## VI. EFFECTS OF MAGIC AND HOW TO OVERCOME THEM

All examples of Christian counseling show the terrible effects of magic. Magic help has to be paid for dearly.

## 3. The Spiritual Weapons.

The Apostle Paul says: "The weapons of our warfare are not carnal, but mighty through God." (II Cor. 10, 4) Every magic procedure can be hindered through believing prayer. Here also is shown the unity of black and white magic. Both react alike towards genuine prayer. A few examples.

E 114   A Christian man got a mesmerizer to attend his sick son. The believing father prayed inwardly, that Christ should prevent the healing, if the man should work with wrong powers. The mesmerizer came, looked at the patient and explained spontaneously: "I cannot help here."

E 115   A man had bone tuberculosis which was charmed according to the manner of white magic. After the charming the pains ceased immediately. The man engaged himself in various forms of magic. He kept many magic books in his house, for instance: 'The Seven Locks of Heaven', 'The Blessing of Tobias' 'The Letter of Protection from John' 'Chainletters' and 'Lucky Letters'. He even carried such letters of protection around with him sown inside his clothes. One day in his great psychic need he sought the way to Christ. He tried to pray but could not. On one hand he had a great desire to come to Christ, on the other hand Christ and the Word of God were violently repugnant to him. This need led to a counseling session during which he handed over all of his magic books. Afterwards he clearly experienced relief and relaxation in his psychic condition.

E 116   A woman with church affiliations suffered from depressions. During one attack she cut her veins. She was found in time by neighbors who called a doctor immediately. She was saved through blood transfusions. After this incident the woman visited a friend of mine who advised her to consult a believing Christian doctor. Since the trip to this doctor was inconvenient she asked another elder for advice. This peculiar Christian directed the woman to a magic charmer. The woman followed his advice and went to the magic healer. This quack told the astonished woman: "I cannot help in your case. Too many people are praying for you. When the people stop with their intercession you can come back again. Then I will be able to make you well." This was reported to me by my friend and he added that he and his wife have been praying for this depressed woman for a long time.

E 117   An occultist wanted to hold an evening meeting with occult experiments. The Christian local minister asked for a few like-minded men. They attended the meeting and prayed during the demonstration. That evening the occultist's experiments were unsuccessful. Finally the man explained excitedly that there were interferences and countercurrents present. The trouble makers should leave the room. The Christian believing men stayed for they had payed for their tickets. This occult experimental lecture therefore proved unsuccessful.

E 118   A Christian couple lived in a house of a woman who engaged in the black art. The woman magician declared one day, she knew how one could get rid of people without them being aware of it. This black magician carried on magic experiments in which she tried to influence and trouble people which she did not like. When the Christian family put their lives completely under the protection of Christ this black magician was infuriated because she could no longer influence these people.

E 119   A paralyzed engineer was treated by a magic charmer. Two of his believing sisters prayed much for the healing of their brother. The charmer could not succeed with his treatment and declared: "I cannot help you. Somebody is praying for you."

These examples show the fact that genuine prayer hinders magic and that magically treated people are disturbed in prayer and faith. Magic can be warded-off then with the spiritual weapons of the Bible.

4. The Deliverance through Christ.

Psychiatrists, psychotherapists, psychologists are not qualified for the treatment of magically subjected people. Magical subjection is not a medical or psychological problem but a Biblical, counseling fact. Relief and deliverance is only possible through Christ. Only when the subjected person wants to come to Christ is genuine and complete help possible.

E 120   A lady missionary M.S. became acquainted with a girl in a Christian boarding house, who in her youth had subscribed herself to the devil. The director of the house told the missionary that she could not handle this girl. The missionary asked the girl to her room and together they started the battle. Her counseling care and intercession led to a complete deliverance of the possessed girl.

E 121   A young man courted a girl of a higher social class. Normally he would have had little hope of success. To reach his goal he subscribed himself with his blood to the devil. He cut his finger, wrote a contract with his blood and left the piece of paper in a cave. In this way he tried to get the power for love magic. A short time after this blood subscription he became scared. He wanted to annul the contract, went to the cave, but could not find the blood contract. The girl accepted his proposal and they enjoyed a very happy marriage. She was an exceptionally pretty young woman. When she delivered twins, the two children were terribly disfigured. The woman was frightened to death and died in childbed. Since the blood subscription the man had not had peace at any time. In his distress he finally sought counseling help. He made a general confession, renounced all dark powers and turned his life over to Jesus Christ. After his conversion he was a living witness for Christ. One and a half years after this change he could enter eternity in peace with God.

E 122   A girl married a man who brought the 6th and 7th Book of Moses into the marriage. During her marriage the young wife suffered from an anxiety state. She saw spooks and at night she often felt as if an unseen power wanted to squeeze her throat. The husband was a bad tempered tyrant. He beat his wife. When she expected a baby he forced her to bring on a miscarriage with the help of tablets. He demanded perverse things from his wife. Finally the young woman wanted to put an end to her suffering. She took eight sleeping pills and ammonia to end her life voluntarily. But she was saved from death. Then she came for counseling help and received assurance of salvation.

E 123   For many years a woman lived at a magic charmer's house. During the nights she was often frigthened by strange spook incidents. Often a black figure appeared or she observed snakes in her room. In her fear and psychic distress she came for Christian counseling. In faith she gave her life to Christ. Each night she put herself consciously under divine protection. From this time on the spook phenomena disappeared completely.

E 124   The wife of a dean was emotionally disturbed. Besides she exhibited various mediumistic faculties. She had visual and acoustic hallucinations. A Christian girl came to take care of this sick woman. The girl started to intercede for the woman. Gradually she gained the impression that the patient was not only emotionally disturbed but also occultly subjected. As the woman had another attack one day the girl commanded the dark powers to leave in the Name of Jesus. Immediately the patient became quiet.

E 125   A Christian woman interceded for a woman suffering from depressions. Afterwards the depression completely left the woman. She became a happy person. But from that time on the woman who had prayed for her had strange experiences at night. She had the feeling that somebody was in the room who wanted to kill her. Her whole body shook and she was terribly frightened. Finally she prayed to Christ and commanded the powers of darkness to leave in the Name of Jesus. The sinister powers left and she had no more trouble in the future.

E 126   The well known man of God Alfred Zeller, the founder of the Maennedorfer Institutions was asked for advice by a woman. Every night from 12 to 1 o'clock her child was plagued and screamed terribly. Zeller questioned the woman about the care of the child, whether the child was hungry or dry or cold, whether it had digestive upsets and so forth. He could not share the woman's conviction that this was caused by magic persecution. Because the woman kept coming to him he finally went to her house and prayed for the child under laying on of hands. While Alfred Zeller prayed the door opened and a dark, heavy-set man with a stabbing look entered. Without greeting he asked: "What is going on here?" Zeller looked at the intruder. At the same moment he was hit by a scathing look of the sinister stranger. Zeller prayed quietly and returned the stabbing look of the man. It came to a spiritual duel. Both men did not let go with their eyes. Inwardly Zeller prayed: "Jesus is victor." The staring look of the stranger broke. Zeller had been victorious by calling on Jesus Christ. The stranger hurried away. A few weeks later it was reported that he had drowned himself in the lake.

All these counseling examples show that Christ overcomes the effects of magic completely. "If the Son therefore shall make you free, ye shall be free indeed." "For this purpose the Son of God was manifested, that he might destroy the works of the devil." (1 John 3, 8). "Christ has delivered us from the power of darkness." (Col. 1, 13) How counseling with the individual is done, regarding deliverance, is here only briefly pointed out. The person who only wants to be delivered without coming to Christ does not experience decisive help. Magic subjection is no disease as most psychiatrists say, but the influence of demonic powers. Christian psychiatrists are of the same opinion. To recognize such facts one has to have eyes that have been opened by the Spirit of God. A medical or theological education in itself is not enough. In the process of deliverance a general confession is advisable. Confession is voluntary. I never saw a person who found relief in this field without a confession. A prayer of renunciation of the dark powers is necessary. Under certain conditions the counselor must command in the Name of Christ. The help of a small prayer group for the subjected person is of great importance. Even today there are Christians who fast in support of their intercession. They are on Biblical grounds. (Math. 17, 21) The delivered person must be faithful in the use of the means of grace (Acts 2, 42), Word of God, fellowship of the believers, breaking of bread, prayer. The final victory is of our Lord Jesus Christ.

## C. SPIRITISM

Spiritism has become a threat to the Christian church and to the Christian message. Christian counseling reveals how many people, who call themselves Christians, have been confused with spiritism. Therefore I have compiled my counseling experiences which deal with spiritism. The urgent need of evangelistic work is to give information about these questions, since there are spiritistic circles in all towns. A well known scientifically recognized expert in this field stated once, that in one Swiss city alone there exist 400 spiritistic circles and 200 more in another town. Furthermore worldwide spiritism is estimated to have about 70 million members. The essence of spiritism was revealed to me personally through many counseling sessions with individuals, which allowed me a shocking insight into this anti-Christian movement. In my collection of occult cases, carried on over many years and numbering over 3000 cases, there are many individual examples which make a judgment possible. The scientific side of spiritism is pointed out in my book "Seelsorge und Okkultismus" which reports 137 examples and investigates them scientifically. The criticism about the use of the word 'case' in connection with these investigations may be right. The English language has at this place no other words than 'case' or 'example'. A person with inner troubles is not a 'case' for me, even if this inept expression has to be used.

The word 'spiritism' comes from the Latin: spiritus, the spirit. One understands under this movement the endeavour to communicate with the dead in the spirit world. Historically spiritism can be traced back over thousands of years. We have testimonies about it in the Old Testament (1 Sam. 28; Deut. 18, 11), furthermore there are many clues to it in the history of the Christian church. Most of the material is found in the history of religion and missions. The non-Christian religions, to a large extent, are spiritistically oriented. If spiritism would only be a fact of pagan religions without any further significance to the present kingdom work, then it would not be very important to the counselor to enter into it seriously. Yet in counseling in so-called Christian countries, such a variety of spiritistic forms with a whole complex of psychic troubles is shown, that it becomes a pressing issue of evangelistic work to give enlightenment about these things. During my thirty years as an evangelist I have found in counseling about 16 different kinds of spiritistic practices which can be divided into five main groups as can be seen in the table of contents. For each group an example from counseling will be given, which will then be discussed briefly. In general long scientific explanations will be avoided. They are given in my previously mentioned book. Finally an opinion will be given about these phenomena.

In its essence this chapter is only an exhibit of material, which shall help the reader form his own opinion. In giving these examples the main emphasis is not on establishing to which theory of explanation it belongs. The question is not whether it should be considered from the spiritistic or animistic point of view. It is concerned with revealing spiritual and counseling questions.

## I. PSYCHIC PHENOMENA

In counseling, the evangelist or Christian worker sometimes experiences that people suddenly want to talk about their spiritual experiences, like veridical dreams, apparitions, visions etc. These things should always be a warning to greatest restraint and caution. Without doubt there are experiences caused by the Word and Spirit of God. But genuine experiences in this area are always evidenced by spiritual modesty. He who makes a spiritual sensation out of it, or a spiritual, better un-spiritual show, evidences by this the artificiality of his experience. The observation of evangelistic counseling teaches that unfortunately artificial spiritual experiences are in the majority. Their ratio is about nine to one over the genuine experiences. We live in a world which has turned from God. The evil, the demonic, the satanic has fullest scope. In our time the overwhelming conviction is forced upon the mind that we are living in a special era of revelation of the false prophet of the End Time. With tremendous force and severity the warning of the Apostle Paul is being fulfilled (II Cor. 11, 14—15): "Satan himself is transformed into an angel of light. Therefore it is no great thing if his ministers also be transformed as the ministers of righteousness." In the field of spiritism the truth and actuality of this warning is clearly revealed.

E 127   A student of theology came for counseling and asked for the explanation of a strange experience. He reported that repeatedly he had had a vision of Christ at night. But during these nightly appearances of Christ he always had an uneasy feeling. He felt no joy but only fear. I explained to this theology student that visions of Christ are possible in principle but most of these appearances come from different causes. For instance there are outer projections of a vivid pious imagination. In the field of psychology it is an established fact that eidetics can see their inner images as an optic picture. Furthermore there are various forms of hallucinations. From the world of the Bible we know that genuine visions of Christ have produced a feeling of sinfulness in the person thus blessed. This feeling of being inwardly undone is completely different though from the feeling of being filled with fear. The student immediately comprehended this difference and said, that he did not have a feeling of sinfulness but only of a great fear during these appearances. Thereupon I asked him whether he or his relatives had engaged in occult practices. He admitted that his mother and grandmother were spiritists and practiced glass-moving. With that explanation the character of the so-called visions of Christ was clear to me. It was a mediumistic not a pneumatic phenomenon.

E 128   The great-grandfather of a family was an active spiritist. For years he practiced table-lifting. He thought he could communicate with the dead in this manner. He carried on this occult practice so intensively that psychic disturbances set in. The effects of his spiritistic practice were shown in an intensified manner in his descendants. The oldest son committed suicide. The second son suffered from a persecution mania. The oldest daughter ended in an insane asylum. The second daughter suffered from Parkinson's disease. In the line of the grandchildren it looks exactly alike. One grandson was schizophrenic, one granddaughter suffers from weak nerves and is hypersensitive, she has also strong feelings of inferiority. Another granddaughter leads a disorderly life. She had an illegitimate child. The first great-grandson in this line is a psychopath and delinquent.

From the scientific point of view this example will be judged differently. The psychiatrist will be interested in the question whether the spiritistic practices really were the cause of the ensuing mental and emotional disorders, or whether up to that time there had not existed a latent disposition which had been triggered or at least favoured by the spiritistic activities. The parapsychologist will explain the table-lifting phenomenon as psychic automatism, as an activation of subconscious forces. The Christian counselor is interested most of all in the frequency of psychic disturbances in connection with occult practice.

E 129   A young woman came for Christian counseling. She complained about various psychic disturbances. She was tired of life and suffered from depressions. Often she had terrible fits of temper. Her marriage was disturbed by her frigidity. In her house objective spook was observed. First her husband saw strange figures. But he did not tell his wife about it because he did not want to upset her unneccessarily. Finally she also observed maimed figures at night in their house. During this counseling session I first took note of the previous diseases of this woman. Then I had her tell me of the diseases of her blood relatives and ancestors. But she was the only one with these disturbances. In answer to the question about occult practices she thought for a long time and then came up with the following story: During her youth she had been a member of a Protestant Girl's Group. The minister's wife, who was the leader, used to practice table-lifting with all the girls. It always began with the question: "Ghost are you there?" One knock meant yes, two knocks meant no. When the ghost was willing to answer, a question and answer game began in which all the girls and also the woman who told me this participated. The minister's wife practiced table-lifting for many years till she was paralyzed by a stroke. The confessing woman told me that the girls of the group were afraid to visit the minister's wife because her face had been changed into a terrible grimace by the stroke.

From the scientific point of view this example is of the same kind as E 128. Regarding the stroke I want to report from the survey of over 3000 occult cases that strokes, suicides, fatal accidents and insanity are often observed in occult practitioners.

E 130  The manager of an estate told me that his mother-in-law had the gift of prevision. With the help of glass-moving she could foretell all coming events. During the war she once surprized her family with the following statement: "Hubert dies in Kurland through death from the air." Hubert was a relative. Half a year later this relative was killed by strafing planes. In all bigger decisions this woman got her advice from glass-moving.

For the scientist the question of prevision is a great problem. In "Seelsorge und Okkultismus" I have shown the thirty best known clairvoyance theories. Occasionally a further theory is brought up in modern parapsychological literature. In the area of magic thought one speaks of a magic-astral world-soul. Behind this concept is the idea of the existence of a world interior, in which all outer occurrences have their inner equivalent. The sphere of the world-soul is not governed by our concepts of space and time. Space and time, past, present and future are all on one level. Synchronism rules here. He who knows how to bring his soul into contact with this world-soul can see all distances of space and time on one level of projection. The mystic participation, the mystic union with the world-soul promotes the thus disposed person as it were into a condition of higher intelligence where the space-time limits of our understanding are lifted. — As dazzling as this hypothesis may be, up till now the exact proof of the existence of an ethic neutral world-soul is lacking. Even if one has arrived at the concept of hypostasis (personification of a concept) in the chokma and logos concept (wisdom, Prov. 8, 22; the Word of God, John 1) the leap to the assumption of a world-soul would be perhaps possible but not demonstrable. In the New Testament the situation is much more simple. We find there pneumatic prophecy produced by the Spirit (Acts 21, 10) and demonic soothsaying (Acts 16, 16).

E 131   A simple farm woman felt pain in her right lower arm. At first this pain was treated as rheumatism. One day the woman made the interesting discovery that the pain suddenly subsided when she wrote letters. When in the following days the pain got very intense she always took a pencil for relief and wrote to alleviate the pain. After some time she discovered that she had developed some kind of writing compulsion. She wrote down things which she could not and would not write down in her conscious mind. When she read her unconsciously written mental products she found to her astonishment that they were religious treatises. She brought these Biblical articles to her minister for examination. This theologian was very much surprized about the intellectual products of this woman. What at first had been a harmless game had turned into a definite habit of automatic writing. One day in her notes a spirit named Felix appeared, who announced himself with the following words: "In the Name of the Lord Jesus, our blessed and exalted Lord and Savior." Then he told the woman that she had been chosen by God for special revelations. From now on she would have to bless mankind as a prophetess with these revelations. This simple farm woman had turned indeed into a spiritistic writing medium.

The parapsychologist sees in this example a psychic automatism, a becoming conscious of subconcious contents. Doubtless one does not have to think here at all about a revelation from the realm of the dead or the other world. But if this simple farm woman considers herself afterwards to be a prophetess, who shall bless mankind with her revelations, then she fell prey to the spirit of pride. The case is not one of direct but of indirect demonization.

E 132    A Protestant minister took part in a spiritistic session to examine a speaking medium. The medium went into a trance (a kind of hypnotic deep sleep). The Apostle Paul appeared and preached to the audience. The Apostle was not visible but only spoke through the speaking medium which laid in a trance. The minister followed the sermon of the allegedly present Apostle with the greatest attention. He was very disappointed about the contents. This so-called sermon of Paul had nothing in common with the letters of the Apostle. The sermon seemed to be more of a product of the medium and consisted merely of a few moral aphorisms with Christian trimming. The minister was not at all convinced of these spiritistic goings-on but was of the opinion that it was a case of unconscious fraud.

The philosopher Wundt said once: "The great minds must have turned into imbeciles at their passing into eternity because they speak such dull and trivial stuff when they are cited by medias." With this statement Wundt wanted to express in an ironical manner that he considers the speeches of the cited great minds as products of the medias. For a Biblically thinking person it is self-evident that the Apostle Paul would never appear on the citation of a medium.

E 133  One day in a spiritistic séance a medium was given the task to call and materialize the spirit of the deceased poet Uhland. Actually during the séance a white phantasm appeared. The audience demanded a poem as proof of the phantasm. Instead of reciting a poem the hand of the phantasm snatched a book from the library and tore out a page. Then the ghost hand grabbed a brief case which was in the room, and through the leather took out a pencil, without opening the briefcase. On the page the hand wrote down a few verses and disappeared. The page was left and is still here today. Uhland experts then rushed upon the Uhland verses and looked for this poem but could not find it. The examination of the graphologist proved to be sensational, for he confirmed the ghost writing to be the handwriting of Uhland. Afterwards in Berlin there was even a trial over the ownership of the page. The court awarded the page to the medium. The medium is still the possessor of the page today as I was told by an acquaintance of the medium.

Scientifically seen there is no necessity to hold to a real appearance of Uhland. The building up of phantasms is to be explained today through depth psychology. It shall be briefly explained here. The medium sends out energy and thickens this energy into matter. According to the findings of nuclear physics this change is possible. Matter is nothing else but compressed energy. We see this equation also in the Einstein formula $E = M \cdot c2$. If another comparison from physics may be given, the following shall be mentioned. When an X-ray tube is driven by a million volt then particles and antiparticles develop at the cathode. We have here also the process in which energy, i.e. electro-magnetic waves deposit matter. The third and fourth mediumistic process is subconscious tapping of knowledge contents and psychic modulation, shaping energy turned to matter according to the tapped material. Finally the phantasm is being directed and the appearance of the deceased from the realm of the dead is finished. — Seen from depth psychology it is therefore not at all necessary that the dead have to be troubled. An animistic explanation pointing to man's subconscious power of mind is sufficient for the phenomenon of materialization. But this does not mean that with this rational theory one does justice to all spiritistic phenomena. No, the problems are not that simple. It is not the place here to enlarge on these questions scientifically. Seen from the view of the Christian counselor I observed many symptoms of split personality in connection with materializations. In some cases in the medium as well as in the participants a disintegration of personality is being observed. But in all cases through frequent participation in spiritistic séances, an immunization against the Holy Spirit and all divine things becomes evident. The spiritistic ghost excesses blunt the personality against the powers that flow from the Word of God.

E 134　A man states that he has the clairvoyance ability to search for missing soldiers. A woman who had two sons at the Russian frontier took two photos of the missing sons and visited this clairvoyant. First she gave him one photo. The man concentrated on the photo, put himself into a trance and explained to the waiting woman: "I cannot get into contact with this son. Probably he is no longer alive." Then to check up on him, the woman gave him the second son's picture who had been reportedly killed in battle by his company chief in 1943. The clairvoyant concentrated on this picture and replied: "I can get in contact with this son. I see him in a great stone building, South-East of Moscow. This son will return as a P. O. W. in 1954." The woman did not believe the statements of the clairvoyant, because her son had been reportedly killed in 1943 and had never given a sign of life. Her surprize was the greater when in the beginning of 1954 this reportedly killed son actually returned. Also the other statements turned out to have been correct. For several years this son had been interned in a P.O.W. camp yet not in wooden barracks but in a white stone building. — This clairvoyant had the peculiarity of concentrating on some object of the missing soldier. If the sought person is still alive then he sees his whereabouts.

Seen parapsychologically two lines are running side by side. The clairvoyant works psychometrically i. e. he takes an object of the missing person and starts his search from there. Furthermore he maintains that he can send out his soul over great distances. This ability of excursion of the soul is for instance told about the Laps in Scandinavia and especially about the Tibetans. In Germany it is the

Rosecrucians, part of whose members have and use this ability. Spiritists say that there are people who can send out of their material body an astral body and commission it for special tasks.

With this the round through the main psychic phenomena of spiritism is ended. One shudders in this dark jungle of human aberration in which spiritism has its haunts. How much clearer and lighter is the Word of God with its invitation: "Thou shalt love the Lord thy God with all thy heart with all thy soul and with all thy strength and with all thy mind." All areas of our life, all forces of our soul shall be directed towards Christ.


## II. PHYSICAL PHENOMENA

As in the first part of spiritistic phenomena mainly inner psychic phenomena were reported, the second part will discuss outer psychic manifestations. In telekinesis, levitation and apports the physical laws are overcome, as it were, in an unknown manner. Under telekinesis one understands that something is set into motion at a distance without a visible cause. The word is made up from two Greek words: 'telos' and 'kinein'. Levitation comes from the Latin and means to ease, lift. In the spiritistic usage this expression means a floating in the air of objects or people. The word apport comes from the Latin apportare and means the fetching and disappearing of objects, also through closed rooms and containers. Also in this group belongs the phenomenon of penetration of matter. Examples shall make these strange occurrences clear.

E 135   In a secluded mountain village a spook house was upsetting the inhabitants. In a farmhouse objects sailed through the air as if thrown by an invisible hand. The furniture in the rooms moved around by itself. The spook house was examined by the local minister, the mayor, the police and many officials and curiosity seekers. The happenings could not be completely explained. It was only observed that telekinetic phenomena only happened when a fourteen year old boy was present. For example the teacher observed that a heavy oak wardrobe moved six feet through the room while the boy was standing by.

E 136   In a farm house of an Alpine valley different spook phenomena occurred. It started with knocking signs and scratching noises. Then objects flew through the room without a visible cause. It was peculiar that these flying objects sometimes were thrown in a rectangular manner which cannot be accomplished by a human hand. The spook phenomena became even more complicated. Objects appeared and disappeared in closed rooms and containers. At this stage people became interested to look for the cause of these spook phenomena. A small committee was formed for the purpose of finding out the natural causes of these occurrences.

In this committee was a professor, an electrical engineer and a philologist, who was acquainted with parapsychological phenomena. The committee first observed that the fourteen year old son of the house was a strong medium. In the presence of the three men team he accomplished some astonishing telekinetic feats. The high light of his performance was the lifting and moving of his bed. This levitation phenomenon was repeated many times. The bed was also lifted up when the three men tried with all of their strength to keep it down.

E 137   A country business woman had her silverware stolen. A very young maid, who had a bad reputation, was suspected. The woman called a spiritist for help who had extraordinary abilities. This man was known as a clairvoyant and medium with the ability of materialization and dematerialization. The spiritist went with the woman into the yard of the house and there put himself into a trance. Suddenly there was a strange noise on the roof of the house. The stolen silverware fell down from the roof and landed in the manure heap. The business woman did not know how this apport had been accomplished.

In this example one does not necessarily have to hold to an apport, since a natural explanation is more feasible. Somebody could have thrown the silverware through a roof window into the yard. But the maid had been fired before this time because of an affair with the hired man. But her friend could have returned the stolen goods, because the theft appeared too dangerous to him. Not so simple is the following example, witnessed to by responsible persons.

E 138   A spook case, which I also could examine, caused a great stir. The house was examined by university professors, the police, the criminal police, a Catholic and a Protestant minister, a government official and several curiosity seekers. Over a period of six weeks 135 objects flew through the rooms of this house in an unexplainable manner. All happenings were precisely registered. Among these flying objects were several apports. When the Catholic priest and two other men sat in the kitchen, a glass ball came flying into the room although the windows and doors were closed. The ball fell at the feet of the priest who picked it up. It felt hot and was not damaged. On the ball was a picture of Maria Einsiedel, a Catholic pilgrimage place in Switzerland. Immediately the owner of the house explained: "This glass ball was laying on a piece of furniture in the living room". They investigated and found that it had disappeared from the furniture.

While examining this spook case I made two observations which are often repeated in connection with these spook phenomena. The flying objects always appear in connection with a mediumistic youth. Furthermore magic had been practiced in this house. My first question to the owner of the house was: "Did you or your ancestors ever practice magic or spiritism?" He immediately answered in the affirmative and reported that his father had been a cattle charmer and had conjured away diseases. According to my experiences spontane apports are only seen in the vicinity of a medium and in houses where occult things had been practiced. In the many spook cases which I examined I never found this rule violated.

With this last example we are already on the way to the spiritistic-magical phenomena which shall now be discussed.

## III. SPIRITISTIC-MAGIC PHENOMENA

In thinking over the past examples, specially of materialization, telekinesis, levitation and apports, one can understand that also much disturbance and mischief can be caused by it. An inferior or even criminal person who possesses such a strong mediumistic power can cause much mischief. Many times in counseling I found terrible connections in this field. A spiritistic circle of twenty members who worked with black magic seemed to me the most sinister. They make experiments to see if they can cause psychic harm or even make people ill, who they do not like. A strong medium of this circle for instance, aimed at a minister and declared: "I'll eliminate him. He is going to be sick." Actually this minister had a nervous breakdown and is sick and unable to work for several months already. A few examples shall make these terrible facts clear.

E 139   A young woman reported that for many years she was frigthened by a nightly spook appearance. Usually between 12 p. m. and 1 a. m. she saw a neighbor woman in her bedroom. The young woman always awoke at this appearance and was terribly frightened. This spook was no dream picture but a waking picture. In the village the neighbor woman had the reputation of an evil woman who worked with black magic and plagued people. After the death of this woman magician the young woman's spook phenomena stopped.

E 140   In the night a strong young farmer experienced beatings scenes. He was beaten bloody without being able to observe anybody. The whole village saw him again and again with blue and red stripes.

E 141   A woman came for Christian counseling and complained that she was molested nightly. A black cat would come into her room at night and scratch and bite her. I questioned her about circulatory disturbances, skin excemas, itching or troubles of old age, like arteriosclerosis, but she had nothing. She told me that once such a cat bite had been seen for fourteen days. Once her foot had not shown the usual scratching and biting marks of the cat but a red number three. It appeared as if the number had been tattooed into the leg with a fine needle.

From the spiritistic-magic cases first of all artificial phenomena have to be eliminated. We know enough psychiatric illnesses in which ideas of reference play a role. For instance many schizophrenics say that they are under some influence or that they are being persecuted magically. In reality this is only a symptom in the course of the psychotic disease. But in the area of spiritistic magic there are also genuine phenomena. I have at my disposal for study an extensive first hand collection of examples. One frequently finds in this connection, that people are beaten by an invisible attacker. In most cases the psychiatric explanation of severe hysteria or onerogenic disturbances or psychogenically caused dermographism is not sufficient. The main argument against these psychiatric explanations is that these strange molestations stop as soon as the victim turns over his life to Christ and places himself under the protection of the blood of Jesus. I have described such an example in my booklet "Jesus lives". Seen from parapsychology, magic persecution is a mediumistic problem in the area of materializations. As the strong medias send out energy with which to build up human phantasms, the medias are also able to transform the sent out energy into animal phantasms. I have collected many materialization cases into dogs, cats, frogs, snakes, or human bodies with animal heads. The following observation proved that first of all it concerns the phenomenon of materialization. In spiritistic séances, it was established, that all injuries that were inflicted upon a phantasm strike back at the medium. It is a significant observation also that injuries which are inflicted upon an animal phantasm, strike back likewise at the medium. Therefore the conclusion is justified that the cases of magic persecution are first of all a phenomenon of materialization. Numerous magic defensive customs are based on this fact. If the victim is able to injure a phantasm which is molesting him, then he has won the battle. We see then that there is spiritistic offensive and defensive magic based on materializations. Following an example.

E 142    In an area where black magic was practiced frequently, I was told the following. At the birth of a child a large black cat wandered around the house. The animal was persistent, it could not be chased away. Finally somebody threw an axe after it. The animal was hurt on the leg. The next day it was discovered that an old woman of the neighborhood had hurt her foot. It was known in the village that the woman was a master of the black art. A few days after this occurrence she took revenge. She visited the mother of the new-born child and patted the child's head murmuringly. From this time on the child cried without ceasing and could not be pacified. Later it was found that the child suffered from a definite weakness of memory.

In my file I have about thirty such cat examples, almost all of which deal with the same problem. In most cases it concerns a person causing house and stable spooks. These are all things of which one knows little or nothing in our universities, which are still under the ban of rationalism. The people are much better oriented about magical customs than our university graduates, who are mostly disciples of the all-leveling humbug and swindle theories.

In Christian counseling the main emphasis is that the magically assailed person places his life under the protection of Christ. That is the only possible and effective help for Christians. The weapons of our warfare are spiritual and not carnal, says the Apostle. — We now turn to another form of the spiritistic catalogue, which is much more complicated to interpret and explain than the phenomena reported so far.


## IV. METAPHYSICAL PHENOMENA

In this group part of the apparition problem and objective spooks in connection with spiritism shall be discussed. The apparition phenomenon is many-sided. There are here, as in all occult manifestations, genuine and artificial phenomena. To the artificial form belongs the outer projection of the eidetic person. Naturally all hallucinations coupled with visions of apparitions fall under this heading. Furthermore visions of apparations as a result of the faculty of second sight belong in this group. Genuine apparition phenomena are the cases which have been objectively confirmed through several generations. An example of this kind shall make the matter clear.

E 143   A university graduate, son of a Protestant minister, told me the following experience in his parent's home. One day the father was transfered to a small town. After they moved into the manse one night the family saw spook phenomena. They heard steps from the cellar into the attic and back and also from the hall into one room. At first these were thought to come from a burglar. Once the police was called. Beside these steps the light was turned on sometimes throughout the house and the gas was also turned on. All careful investigations turned up no evidence as to the cause of these spooky occurrences. When the older sons of the manse were college students they thought of a plan to contact this nightly disturber of the peace. One night the students sat with their parents around a table, formed a chain with their hands and tried to contact this ghost by table-lifting. First they asked: "Are you a spirit that cannot find rest?" The question was answered by a violent rapping on the table. Thereupon an interesting question-and-answer game started. The invisible one, with whom they had made contact, stated that he was a Catholic priest who had lived in this house 200 years ago. He had murdered his housekeeper and buried her in the basement. Since that time he had to haunt the place of his crime. Following the question, in which room he had murdered the housekeeper, a strange phenomenon began. The table slid through the room to the door and hit the door so hard that the wood was knicked. As one of the students opened the door the table whizzed into the adjoining room and slid into the corner. The table hit an oak bed and the impact left deep marks which never disappeared. In reply to the question whether they could do something for him, he answered: "Yes, pray." After the minister's wife prayed for the restless ghost, the haunted house enjoyed peace for a few years. One of the sons, Dr. X. my reporter told me that he had made investigations and found out that actually 200 years ago the house had been inhabited by a Catholic priest. The spook had been observed through many generations. The minister's families who moved out kept silent about their experiences in the house, in order not to frighten the families that were moving in. It is interesting to note that after this particular minister's family moved out, the spook started again with his successor.

There are several interpretations for the phenomenon of apparitions. Martensen Larsen believes that man spiritually impregnates his home. This impregnation, as a psychic leftover would continue to live an independent existence. Prof. Gatterer believes that man does not only leave his material body but also a spiritual larva. Prof. Bender speaks only about a whirl which is caused by the departing person. The spiritualists believe that man does not only leave his body on this earth but also a spiritual complex which keeps existing independently in the astral world and sometimes disintegrates only after centuries. This spiritual complex causes the phenomenon of apparitions and locality-bound objective spook. From the Christian side comes the opinion that we should not imagine the realm of the dead as a place, but as a condition, a state of being. There are moments in which this realm of the dead which surrounds us, becomes transparent, for instance on the deathbed or in mediumistic people. From the Christian Theosophy of Hahn and Oetinger comes the idea that a conative, earth-bound human being has to move in the mortal sphere after his death till he is freed from the things that bind him. This idea is the same as the popular opinion that criminals or evil doers have to haunt the place of their crime till they are taken out of this sphere, according to the principle of upward or downward development. All these theories are very shaky, for we have no unequivocal passage in the Bible in explanation of apparitions. To avoid misunderstandings it must be said here that there are of course apparitions not only in the spiritistic realm. The problem was only briefly discussed in connection with example E 143, since the contact with the ghost was made through spiritistic table lifting.

E 144    After moving to a new location a preacher and his wife both observed strange spook phenomena in the house where they were living. At night they always heard steps moving through the house. From Easter Saturday till Easter Sunday they heard knocking and crashing noises, as if all the furniture was being smashed. They thought of burglars and went to investigate. But nothing had been changed in the room. Later they heard knocking signs. The spook phenomena were also observed by guests, who had not been initiated. Sometimes the guests were molested during the day as well as at night time. The preacher and his wife prayed without ceasing to win out over these disturbances. Finally he dared to command in the Name of Jesus these invisible disturbers of the peace. One morning before dawn they heard that all bricks were being tapped. Afterwards there was a noise as if hundreds of pigeons were flying away. The preachers family had the impression that the spook had come to an end. This was true, for the house stayed free from that day on. While investigating the possible causes, the preacher found out that many years before them a spiritist had lived in the house. Furthermore a suicide had been committed in the house a few years before the preacher moved in.

When I was asked for advice and help in objective spook cases, I always made two observations which repeated themselves constantly. Objective spook has its cause in the occult activity of the ancestors. The appearance of the objective spook is more persistent than the person-bound spook, but he also retreats immediately when the inhabitants completely commit themselves to Christ and place themselves under His protection. This is a sign that these are not only scientifically explainable occurrences, but that they have a metaphysical background.


## V. CULTIC PHENOMENA

In showing the easily perceptible experiments of spiritism one can meet with the following reproach: "We do not engage in such low forms of spiritistic appearances. We are interested in spiritual, noble things, in spiritualism." Once a man who had been a spiritualist for many years told me that he personally holds spiritism to be a crime.

What about this question? As a matter of fact the spiritistic movement has been succeeded by a more spiritual higher form of spiritism, namely spiritualism. While spiritism of the old kind is more concerned with massive experiments, spiritualism wants a spiritual and religious expansion of their ideas. Without doubt spiritualism has a much higher level intellectually and ethically than spiritism of the old kind. We find pronounced forms of spiritualism for instance in Switzerland in the Spiritual Lodge in Zurich. Recently also in Winterthur a Christian-Spiritistic Association was formed. This lodge in Zurich has a worship service each Sunday with songs, prayer and sermon. The sermon is allegedly given by a spirit from the other side who speaks through a medium. The sermons are being taken down in shorthand and published each week. I have read several of these sermons. They contain idealistic, moral and Christian thought. Their main message is below the level of the New Testament. These spiritualistic sermons fall short in bringing the centre of the Christian message that before God man is a poor, lost sinner and needs redemption through Jesus Christ. Beside this critical observation it should be added that the spiritualists give a new interpretation to New Testament events. The resurrection accounts, also the resurrection of Jesus and the appearance of Moses and Elijah on the mount of transfiguration, are being spiritistically understood. Besides this one avoids through a forced exegesis the Words of Scripture which forbid communication with the dead. Once when I cited Deuteronomy 18, 10—12 to a member of the spiritistic movement, that questioning the dead is an abomination to the Lord, he explained to me: "We do not call the dead, but the living spirits from the realm of the dead." All of spiritualism is confusing to people who lack insight because of the Christian accessories.

It is extremely disastrous that even in some Christian circles the spiritistic excesses are not being recognized. Two examples shall show this.

E 145   A Christian family, who are members of a fundamental church experiences strange apparitions. An aunt of this family is a medium. In the evening the members of the family sit together and then through the alleged mediation of the aunt well-known men of God appear from the other side. Tersteegen appears and holds devotions. Michael Hahn, Stockmaier, Samuel Keller and others appear and preach to the assembled family. It is remarkable that these ghost sermons are not above what these men have written in their lifetime, they do not even reach the intellectual level of their writings.

E 146   A believing woman church member lost her husband early in life. She could not console herself over the death of her husband. Then a very strange thing happened. Her deceased husband appeared to her at night and declared that from now on he was allowed to appear to her to console her. The marriage was continued in a spiritual form through the appearance of the dead husband. The woman explained that these appearances were a source of strength for her and a help for the difficulties of the day. In all problems she receives advice and direction from her deceased husband. A well-known Christian counselor advised her to reject the intercourse with the deceased. But the woman was not to be convinced of the objectionableness of her action. It is noteworthy that during the course of communicating with the dead psychic disturbances appeared and her health was slowly being impaired.

It is a sad sign of the lack of proving of spirits that in Christian and even in believing circles the pneumatic and the spiritistic, that is the spiritual and psychic or even demonic cannot be differentiated. To point out that even great men experienced appearances from the dead is no Biblical argument. Our standard is not what great men do but what the Word of God says. When the rich man asked for an appearance from the dead (Luke 16) it was told to him: "They have the Word of God." Markus Hauser, who saw spirits, said that the ability to see spirits was not a gift but a plague to him. And Oberlin was influenced by Swedenborg in his vision of spirits. It was proved that Swedenborg was out of his mind during the periods of his spirit visions. We do not need the confusing light of uncontrollable spirits, but the Word of God alone, which is the carrier of the Holy Spirit. We also do not need religious effusions and products of spiritistic writing medias, as for instance Jakob Lorber and others, but we only need the Spirit of Truth, which opens up the Word of God. The expansion of spiritism into a religious cult is perhaps the most dangerous form of this movement because naive souls are blinded and confused by the Christian accessories. With this we are faced with the problem of judging spiritistic phenomena.

# VI. JUDGING SPIRITISTIC PHENOMENA

1. Let neutral science speak first. In medicine, specially in psychiatry one knows about symptoms of split personality which are produced by prolonged activity with mediumistic forces. It is defined as mediumistic psychosis. Psychology also has clearly judged mediumistic experiments. The warning of a psychologist shall follow here. Prof. Bender of the University of Freiburg writes in his booklet "Parapsychology — its results and problems": 'Thousands of people put their hopes in the deceptive proclamations of spiritistic practitioners, receive advice from the other side and become dependent upon it. I have seen quite a number of patients who have suffered serious psychic disturbances through the misuse of such practices. They have become split personalities. The spirits which they called, confused them. He who tries to discover the promises of the other side through superstition endangers himself to fall prey to the dark side of his psyche."

2. The Biblical classification of spiritism is clearly pointed out in a few Scripture passages. In Lev. 20, 27 it is written: "And a man also or woman that hath a familiar spirit, or that is a wizard, shall surely be put to death: they shall stone them with stones." Before entering the promised land the children of Israel received this warning from God, Deut. 18, 9—12: "When thou art come into the land which

the Lord thy God giveth thee, thou shalt not learn to do after the abominations of those nations. There shall not be found among you one that uses divination, or an observer of times, or an enchanter or a witch, or a charmer, or a consulter with familiar spirits, or a wizard or a necromancer. For all that do these things are an abomination unto the Lord." What was valid in Moses' time also continued into the time of the kings. Saul had prohibited all fortune telling and spiritism, till after his apostasy from the living God he gave himself to spiritistic things. (1. Sam. 28) He got his own death sentence through the spiritistic medium of Endor. The time of the prophets was no different than the period of Moses and the kings. Isaiah defended himself against fortune tellers and diviners with the challenge (8, 19): "Should not a people seek unto their God? Or shall we ask the dead for the living?" Spiritism is a crime against the sovereignty and authority of God, a transgression of the First Commandment. The spiritists leave the living God and follow confusing lights and scintillating spirits which nevertheless lead them astray. A tragic example shall show this.

E 147  A Protestant minister was a member of a spiritistic circle for years. His sixteen year old son also took a regular part in these séances. When his son fell behind in school he was given a job as book-keeper of this spiritistic association. Often spiritistic thought entered his Sunday sermon. He would say for instance: "The Holy Spirit, that is the good attribute in us." Regarding the leading of the Spirit he completely represented the spiritistic line. He told his congregation that there are good spirits on the other side which have a direct influence on our daily life and which can lead us. He made no secret of the fact that he was lead and directed by these spirits. One day he had a bad experience in this regard and became the laughing stock of the village. He ordered a buggy from a distant village to take him to the place where his mother lived. The good spirits had told him that his mother had suddenly been taken ill and he would have to hurry in order to see her still alive. The news spread through the village like a prairie fire that the minister's mother was dying. An hour after the buggy's departure the mailman brought a letter from the mother which contained the news that she was enjoying the best of health. Immediately the minister's wife sent a messenger after the buggy to inform her husband. The buggy turned around. The whole village ridiculed this experience. From this time on the minister did not find much faith in his spirit theories on the part of his congregation. One day the minister came to a tragic end. During their vacation he and his wife went to the sea shore. While bathing he told his wife: "I'll swim out now and will never come back." He did and it happened as he had predicted.

This tragic example shows clearly the confusion caused by spiritism. The minister dissolved the Holy

Spirit, the third person of the trinity, into a few moral attributes. He volatilized the person and effect of the Holy Spirit into a few inobligatory human qualities and instead put his spiritistic ghosts on the throne. These 'good spirits' made a fool of him in front of his whole congregation and are probably also responsible for his suicide.

3. In Christian counseling a clear distinction has to be made between the scientific explanations of spiritistic phenomena and the spiritual relationships. The spiritistic problem, as any other occult problem, is two-fold. The material principle of investigation of these phenomena is concerned with scientific illumination. The formal principle of investigation is concerned with bringing these appearances under the spiritual scope of the Holy Scriptures. Ethical and Biblical judging of spiritistic phenomena is completely independent of the scientific interpretation. Even if it should be proved that all spiritistic phenomena are animistic, i. e. to be explained through an action of subconscious psychic powers, still the spiritual counseling problem will remain untouched. Progressive research in depth psychology will not be able to push Christian counseling into retreat since the spiritual sphere of these questions lies on a different dimension.

In Biblical, spiritual regard Christian counseling has shown unequivocally that spiritistic activity is a point of invasion of dark powers. I say a point of invasion; for there are many such points in other areas also. Here the warning of the Apostle Paul takes on special meaning: "For we wrestle not against flesh and blood, but against principalities, against powers, against the rulers of the darkness of this world, against spiritual wickedness in high places" (Eph. 6, 12). In counseling this invasion of dark powers is sometimes quite obvious. There are cases in which the regular reading of spiritistic literature is enough to bring on disturbances in the psychic and religious life. An example follows.

E 148   A young Christian woman received sermons and other literature from a friend of a spiritistic circle. She thought these writings to be Christian literature and read them regularly. She experienced serious temptations and attacks of despondency through this reading. Unsuspectingly she continued to read the literature. Then one night in her room she observed a red-haired man with a glowing face. She also showed compulsive-obsessive trends with a destruction mania. She felt an inner impulse to kill her own child though her mind opposed it violently. In counseling I advised her to immediately burn the spiritistic literature and to consult a psychiatrist.

Of course the psychiatrist will say that compulsion neurosis with devious impulsive actions in a state of clear or disturbed consciousness is a well-known psychiatric picture. Also the hallucinations point to this picture. This psychiatric diagnosis will of course be accepted. It is strange though, that this

illness often follows in the train of spiritistic activity. Even if it should not be maintained that spiritism is the effecting cause, many observations have
shown that it could be the triggering cause. Not
causa efficiens, but causa exsolvens. Regarding the
hallucination of the red-haired man, I like to mention that in the course of reading spiritistic literature, spiritistic visions are likely to appear. Sometimes naive people take such hallucinations to be a
religious experience. This is as far as the confusion
and disguise of the satanic spirits into angels of
light goes. The observation of Christian counseling
confirms the fact that spiritistic activity seriously
harms the Christian's spiritual life. The belief in
Buddha or Mohammed or another of the great lea-
ders of religious history is not being hindered
through spiritistic activity. This is revealing as to
the background. Spiritism immunizes against the
workings of the Holy Spirit. This must not be mis-
understood. It does not harm religious life in general, just the opposite, spiritism in itself is to a great
degree a 'religious' movement. Bluntly said it
means: The devil does not take away our'religiosity' but he wants to hinder us at any cost from becoming followers of Jesus. Therefore when people
from spiritistic circles tell me that spiritism especially has helped them grow in their devotion and
religiosity, then I immediately acknowledge it. But
to be a follower of Jesus and to be born again by the
Holy Spirit is something totally different than reli-

giosity. And there are even in our Christian circles, sad as it is, more 'religious' than believing people. I have had many striking examples about the sharp contrast between spiritism and the Holy Spirit. One case shall be repeated.

E 149  In ignorance a believing man attended a spiritistic séance. Because he felt uneasy, he began to pray silently. The assembled group tried to do table-lifting. It would not succeed. After the believing man had left the room, the table-lifting was successful again.

Another observation of Christian counseling that in enormously many cases psychic disturbances develop from spiritistic activity, does not have to be discussed further. Now I want to close the description of spiritism from the viewpoint of Christian counseling. Some specific forms of spiritism could not be discussed here. But the main forms have been shown. To give the Christian worker a few more directions for Christian counseling, the counseling treatment of a spiritistically subjected person shall be shown in the form of a sketch.

4. Deliverance from the ban of spiritism and spiritualism is only possible through Christ. Every medical or psychological help does not do justice to the spiritual character of this phenomenon. Because of the act of Christ on the cross and on Easter morning, counseling with occultly subjected people is victorious counseling without fear. Satan and all of his cohorts are a defeated army. All occult powers

are made powerless by Jesus. This is the song of triumph of the New Testament: "And Christ, having spoiled principalities and powers, he made a shew of them openly, triumphing over them in it" (Col. 2, 15). What the Old Testament congregation sang: "The right hand of the Lord doeth valiantly" (Psalm 118, 15) was fulfilled in Christ. The Apostle Paul exults: "Thanks be to God which giveth us the victory through our Lord Jesus Christ" (I Cor. 15, 57). The redemption and the victory of Jesus is the background for hopeful counseling and help for the occultly subjected person. In this counseling directive particular attention has to be given to the following points:

a) The person who wants to be delivered must give himself over to Jesus without reservations. There is no half-way solution or half decision. One cannot serve two masters.

b) It has been shown in almost every case that the subject does not come through without a complete confession. In the New Testament confession is a voluntary act. But in over three thousand occult cases I have never seen one who could be delivered without a thorough counseling session. James must have had this experience, because he writes: "Confess your faults one to another" (James 5, 16).

c) There are specially difficult cases in which a prayer of renunciation is necessary. Occult activity is always an often unconscious contract with the darkness. This contract is being called off through the prayer of renunciation in the presence of the counselor who is a witness. This calling off is done only once. It ist not repeated. This renunciation can be put into these words: "In the Name of Jesus Christ I absolve myself from you, Satan and give myself over to Jesus as my Lord." The same words need not be used. In counseling there are no magic charms.

d) In some cases the counselor needs to command in the Name of Jesus. But an expert knowledge and the gift of discerning of spirits is necessary here in order for the commanding not to be misused. It could be wrong to command in a medical case, such as a mentally or emotionally disturbed person. Here grievous mistakes can be made in counseling. It is better in an uncertain case to be cautious than to command. He who commands must be a disciple of Jesus and must place himself in faith under the protection of Jesus. Otherwise it can happen to him that he experiences serious temptations. In general one does not pray by laying on of hands with the occultly subjected person. Jesus laid hands only on sick people while he commanded those that had demons.

e) The delivered person must make diligent use of the means of grace: The Word of God, fellowship of the believers, breaking of bread and prayer (Acts 2, 42). If the temptations return after he had counseling care, he has to put himself daily and hourly under the protection of the blood of Jesus.

This is no emotional blood mysticism but Biblical reality. A fight against the darkness cannot be waged with sentimentality. If the temptations do not cease, the tempted person himself can command in the Name of Jesus. Commanding by people of the world is completely useless, it may be even dangerous, as for instance is shown in Acts 19, 13. Commanding by Christians lacking complete commitment to Jesus has no power. Since the expelled spirits and powers like to return to their old habitation (Luke 11, 24—26) the delivered person has to be on guard. The spiritual armor (Eph. 6, 10—18) is necessary. The most important weapon is "the shield of faith and the sword of the Spirit, which is the Word of God." Coming from spiritism a person has to be on guard against all experiences and visions. The returning spirits often sneak in under pious camouflage. They are often not recognized in their religious disguise.

f) There are difficult cases in which counseling does not lead to a complete and immediate liberation. There are two possibilities of special help. In most cases a prayer circle of two or three believers must be formed who meet together at least twice a week for prayer and intercession. The subjected person is taken into this circle. Intercession is kept up until deliverance takes place. A small prayer circle has more spiritual authority than the single counselor. The promise is theirs: "If two of you shall agree on earth as touching any thing that they shall ask, it shall be done for them of my Father which is in heaven" (Math. 18, 19). The second form of special help is praying and fasting. Jesus says in Math. 17, 21: "This kind goeth not out but by prayer and fasting." The small prayer circle together with the subjected person or in this case also without him can hold prayer-and-fasting days. But the praying people must guard against the thought of gain or a pharisaical performance. He who stands in the front line battle with the powers of darkness must be armed against the wiles and attacks of the enemy. Many a prayer warrior and Christian worker came to fall in such a battle. Over the path of spiritual pride it often leads to gross sins.

g) Attention should be paid to cases which show symptoms of psychiatric illness and a specialist should be consulted. In this area the counselor must not turn into a psychiatric quack.

After the many reports of spiritistic subjection three deliverance examples shall constitute the end.

E 150    A young spiritist had made experiments according to the instruction of the 13 Books of Moses. They are magic books which have nothing to do with Moses. He wanted to try out the charms to see if they worked. Many things succeeded but others did not. One day he gave the order according to the magic books to call for the money spirit. He drew a magic circle, drew the magic symbols inside the circle and used the charm of invocation three times. Of course the money spirit did not appear but after the invocation he fell down in the magic circle and was unconscious for a long time. For weeks he laid as if paralyzed and had no physical or will power. All joy of life had left him. In this condition he turned to Christ. After many counseling sessions and the support of a prayer circle he was delivered by Christ. Today he is a faithful follower of Jesus.

E 151   A young woman accepted a friend's invitation to attend a spiritistic circle. In the beginning this circle gave her satisfaction till she observed on herself increasingly psychic changes. She suffered from depressions which caused her to consult a neurologist. During the course of the treatment she was committed to a mental hospital. Because she was limited in her freedom, she could no longer attend spiritistic séances. Her condition improved. Christian counseling by the chaplain helped her complete her recovery. The woman opened herself to the influence of the Word of God. She learned to believe in Christ and decided to follow Him. After a few weeks she was released as cured. She stayed well permanently.

E 152   During one of my many evangelistic trips in Switzerland I followed the inner development of a woman who had carried on almost all forms of spiritism and magic. Her mother had charmed her magically before her birth and later as a child she was healed of diseases through magic. The parents instructed their growing daughter in the magic practices. All known forms of magic like black magic, white magic, magic persecution, magic defence, fortune-telling, card laying, palmistry, necromancy etc. were tried out in experiments. After her marriage the young woman continued these black arts until one day she was disturbed in this activity. During a nightly séance she suddenly heard rattling of chains, crashing and knocking noises. She also felt that her bed was being lifted up repeatedly. She asked herself whether these were signs of a mental illness or effects of black magic. In this time of trouble she started to read the Bible and pray. But every time she tried she had great difficulties. This gave her the thought that she was dealing with dark powers. She confided in a Christian woman acquaintance. A small prayer circle started interceding for her. The inner development of the woman went up and down. She was torn between faith and doubt. She longed for peace with God and yet could not get rid of feelings of fear. The tremendous battle lasted for two years. Finally she saw a vision. A bowl of blood was passed down from heaven to her. She thought at once: "This is the blood of Christ, which has been shed for me also." From this time on she could believe the Word of God. Her temptations ceased. Through Christ she experienced complete deliverance. Today the woman has the desire to praise daily the blood of Jesus Christ as a sign of her redemption.

This presentation of the spiritistic dangers shall

end with the glad tidings: The Gospel is the great message of victory of the most successful battle in world history. The cross of Golgotha is the great reminder of the victory and of the liberation from all powers of darkness. He who comes to the cross partakes of the victory of Jesus Christ.

# D. OCCULT LITERATURE

Magic books are like poisonous vapours that circulate among the people and poison their souls. To name all of these publications would make a giant list. Therefore only those shall be named which circulate in Germany and Switzerland. Some of the best-known titles are: Romanus Booklet, Secrets of Nigromantiae, The Real Fiery Dragon, The Reign over the Spiritis of Heaven and Hell, The Book of Venus to Conjure Evil Spirits. Also the books of the mystic and spiritualist Jacob Lorber belong to occult literature, then the writings of the apostate Catholic priest Greber, as well as the writings of the Spiritualistic Lodge in Zurich. The principal work of magic in Europe is the so-called 6th and 7th Book of Moses. It is a tragedy that this book is still being printed and published. Several court trials were waged against its distribution but without success. This chapter about the main book of magic was a legal opinion for the Attorney General who had started legal proceedings against the publishers of the book. He who is not interested in the history should at least read the examples to get an idea of the danger of this book.

## 1. History

During the last twenty years many people with whom I counseled turned over to me their copies of this book. The oldest edition which was turned over to me comes from the year 1503. In the preface it was written that this book had been published under the protectorate of a Pope. These dubious statements would have to be verified for their truthfulness. In the preface of another edition of this notorious magic book it is noted that a monk from Erfurt collected these magic charms. Seperate editions of the last four hundred years differ widely in their contents.

In the 19th century the 6th and 7th Book of Moses was mixed with parts of a French magic book "The Fiery Dragon". This French book is supposed to have been printed at the end of the 17th century from a manuscript of the year 1522. After the French Revolution of 1789 which wanted to dethrone God and enthrone the goddess of reason, "The Fiery Dragon" became the sinister substitute Bible of French magic circles. We have here a frequent occurence in religious history. He who repudiates the living God falls prey to the devil. The belief in God was succeeded in turn by a terrible subjection to the devil. After the merger of parts of these two magic books, the double books were published, partly under the name "The Fiery Dragon" or "The Sixth and Seventh Book of Moses" or under a collective title "Magic-Sympathetic House Treasure."

The title "6th and 7th Book of Moses" is a pseudonym, a deceitful cover name. Moses has nothing to do with these magic charms. The magicians have only elevated Moses as their patron and master since his victorious battle with the Egyptian magicians (Exodus, Chapters 7—8). This is a diabolic misunderstanding of the prophetic endowment of this Old Testament Man of God. In recent years the 6th and 7th Book of Moses has had a new edition. A publisher in Braunschweig has the sorry distinction of distributing this terrible book. Copies have been handed over to me which look like a New Testament in form and make-up.

## 2. Distribution of the book

During the last years I have given lectures of information about the dangers of occultism in all of the German speaking areas, i. e. Germany, Switzerland, Austria, Alsace and the Saar area. I also spoke in German communities in foreign countries like Spain, Italy, the Balkan, England and the Skandinavian countries. An extensive occult literature is to be found in all European countries. The 6th and 7th Book of Moses exists in all German-speaking parts of our continent. During 110 weeks of lecturing in Switzerland I found special areas of circulation in Canton Appenzell and St. Gallen (Toggenburg) also in Graubuenden. It is also to be found in lesser numbers in all other parts of Switzerland. In the Austrian Alpine valleys, in Alsace and Lorraine it is to be found in greater numbers. In Germany the main areas are the central Black Forest, the Swabian Alp, the Bavarian Alpine valleys, the central German mountains, the Lueneburg heath, Mecklenburg and Sleswick-Holstein. As in Switzerland the book is to be found in lesser numbers in all other parts of Germany. It is rarely to be found in new industrial settlements. The German settlements on the Balkan were completely infested with this book. The settlers who immigrated to Germany still carry on their magic customs.

## 3. Contents

A detailed summary of contents is not necessary here and not advisable. Directions are given in the book, as to how man can get in touch with the devil. There are charms for magic persecution and magic defence, forms of vengeance magic, illness magic, death magic, fertility magic, love magic and many more. Many charms are camouflaged with religious trimmings. To those who want to read and keep the book for the sake of study, it must be told, that in the 6th Book chapter 6, Satan's special protection is promised to those who read and own the book.

## 4. Examples

A few examples from my files shall follow. They are chosen at random and can be supplemented by many more.

E 153   For years a man worked with the 6th and 7th Book of Moses. His wife also took part in occult practices. The descendants of this family suffer from nervous and psychic disorders. One daughter had the feeling as if a wall existed between her and

God. She turned to Christ but did not experience a complete deliverance from her psychic troubles. A granddaughter of this family was a deaconess. She also felt a wall between her and God and became emotionally disturbed. The medical superintendent of a psychiatric clinic told her: "Your sickness does not fit into the psychiatric picture."

E 154   A mother knew a few strong charms to get rid of warts and skin diseases. She used her art on her own children. Her children are occultly subjected. One daughter was a schizophrenic, the mother herself suffers from blasphemous thoughts and depressions. In reply to the question where she had learned her occult arts, she stated that her husband had brought the 6th and 7th Book of Moses into the marriage. From that time on strange new things had appeared in her life. The way to Christ was shown to her and she actually was freed. On the day of her conversion there was a tremendous crashing and knocking noise in the whole house as if it were filled with evil spirits. Through the grace of God the mother is now delivered. But her children are still subjected to these occult powers.

E 155   A man learned black magic with the help of the 6th and 7th Book of Moses. He engaged in magic persecution as well as magic defence. He supported his magic practices with symbolic actions. He thought to protect himself from persecution by sticking an open knife into a table. He tried to plague his enemies by locking urin into a bottle while murmuring a magic charm. Through this magic act his enemies were supposed to be unable to urinate.

E 156   For many years a man practiced the black art with the help of the 6th and 7th Book of Moses. Shortly before his death he turned over his book to his oldest son and instructed him in the magic rules. The son continued the dark business of his father. From the third generation on all descendants suffered from melancholy. The two daughters of the black magician and all of his grandchildren have tendencies to depression.

E 157   For many years a man worked with the 6th and 7th Book of Moses and made experiments in the field of black magic. The effects of this magic practice are clearly seen in his house and descendants. For years all inhabitants of the house heard knocking signs. At night there were such rumbling and crashing noises that people who stayed overnight were frightened. The descendants of this occult practitioner have abnormal characteristics. The son was a brutal, quick-tempered man who harrassed his first wife to death. He also plagued the second wife inhumanly for many years. He is a furious tyrant who also mistreats children. All of his children had left home before their twentieth year because of the father. The diligent, patient wife suffers terribly from her husband.

E 158   All of his life a man had engaged in black magic with the help of the 6th and 7th Book of

Moses. The home and family of this man is a place of unrest and discord. The occult practitioner died a terrible death under agonizing pains while spreading a penetrating stench. His wife poisoned herself and died also under horrible pains. One son died in his youth. The daughter has serious psychic troubles. As an adult she is still a bed-wetter, suffers persistently from sexual troubles and emotional disorders. The house of this family is plagued by spook phenomena. Knocking signs and rattling noises are to be heard in the house. At night apparitions can be seen also.

E 159   On her deathbed a woman wanted to give her oldest son the 6th and 7th Book of Moses. The son refused to take it. The line of descendants of this woman who had engaged in black magic for many years, included many psychically abnormal members. Melancholy, quarrelsomeness, irascibility and other extreme dispositions belong to the emotional and mental characteristics of the descendants.

E 160   The grandfather of a farm family owned the 6th and 7th Book of Moses and used it for his magic arts. All of his descendants are abnormal. Two daughters are constantly running to fortune-tellers and both have emotional disturbances. When the old black magician died spook phenomena appeared in the house. A man without head was repeatedly observed in the house. Also the line of grandchildren shows different disorders. One grandchild always fell out of bed at night. A magic defence charm was used and from that time on the child stayed in bed. Other grandchildren of the magician are cleptomaniacs and sexual delinquents. A great-grandson of this man who is only fourteen years old has already nervous disorders.

E 161   In a house the 6th and 7th Book of Moses was kept and used for years. The children of this family are all abnormal. One daughter suffers from depressions. One son is an alcoholic and sex offender.

E 162   I know four ministers, also a Seventh Day Adventist preacher who keep the 6th and 7th Book of Moses in their library for orientation. It is a noteworthy observation that Christian workers who keep such literature in their library usually have a spiritually dead congregation.

E 163   A preacher of a church works under much difficulty. He is known for shepherding a totally lame and spiritually dead congregation. After a lecture of information about the occult field, this preacher confessed that for years he had been interested in occult literature and that he keeps all magic books, also the 6th and 7th Book of Moses.

E 164   A Sunday School teacher practiced table-lifting for many years. She also occupied herself with the 6th and 7th Book of Moses and used charms against sicknesses. In counseling I found out that many people of her circle of acquaintances were occultly subjected by her.

E 165   In the year 1946 a young farmer took over

the farm of his father. In the fall of the same year all of his pigs died. Since the veterinarian could not find any cause of death, the farmer sent a whole pig to the Animal Biological Institute at Zurich for examination. Every known test for poisoning was made on the body of the animal. The tests were unsuccessful. The cause of the animals death could not be discovered. When in the fall of the following year suddenly all of the animals died again, the farmer made even greater efforts to find out the cause of death. The stables were inspected, the fodder was probed, the dead pigs again were examined. All efforts were unsuccessful. Thereupon he had the pigsty torn down and rebuilt with new wood at another site. In the third year the pigs died again. The animals shrieked suddenly and then collapsed. All examinations were repeated. The farmer's brother fed the left-over fodder to his own pigs without any ill effects. The farmer was told from different sides: "You must have an enemy who plagues and kills your animals magically." At first the farmer rejected such advice as pure nonsense. He consulted the veterinarian who knew no other help in view of the frequency of the accidents. Regarding the question of magic the victim turned to the local minister who simply laughed at him with the remark: "There are no such things." A few of his fellow villagers pointed out to him, that there were black artists in Canton Toggenburg who could also kill pigs, cattle and horses through magic. This continued year after year. The farmer secured his stables with double locks. At night he stretched a black thread all around his house in order to see if anyone was gaining entrance into the house. The stables were models of hygiene. The fodder was carefully controlled, the breeding stock was repeatedly changed. All efforts always had the same results. In the fall, as well as before the high holidays like Christmas and Easter, the pigs always died suddenly.

One day this mysterious affair took a strange turn. The local minister visited the farmer and asked him to accompany him to have a talk together. His neighbor, who had a bad reputation in the village, had confessed something to him, and now wanted to repeat this confession in the presence of the farmer and ask him for forgiveness. The three men sat together in the study of the minister. The ill-reputed neighbor stated that he had killed the farmer's pigs each year with the help of black magic. In the meantime there had been 32 pigs in all which had died in this strange manner. The farmer was indignant about this and asked him why he had done it. The neighbor explained: "I always got angry at your children who made such noise near my house." The minister then asked the confessor how he was able to do these things. In reply to this question the man made the following statement: As a young man he had gotten hold of several magic books, among them 6th and 7th Book of Moses.

He studied this occult literature diligently and learned in it about the so-called devil's pacts or devil's subscriptions. Finally he had the desire to try out this strange experiment once. During a Friday night between 12 p. m. and 1 a. m. he went to a crossroad and there subscribed himself with his own blood to the devil. He explained that a regular contract had been drawn up between him and the devil. During this act he had seen the devil personally but not like the medieaval conception with horns, tail and goat-feet but as a figure with black, curly hair, blood-red eyes and a small snout. He was dressed in black in an old-fashioned style. From that day on this clever pupil of the 6th and 7th Book of Moses in partnership with the devil, had occult abilities which he used to kill the 32 pigs. The minister then asked the confessor, why he had relieved his conscience now. He told him that over the years his neighbor had been so good to him that he felt ashamed. He then promised that from now on he would spare the farmer with this stable spook. The farmer did not want to turn the man in because in such a case there are no legal evidences. From the time of the confession for the next six months the neighbor with the magical ability attended church. During that time none of the farmer's pigs died. After half a year the man backslid, started to drink again and stayed away from church. Before the Day of Prayer and Repentance, two of the farmer's pigs died again in the same manner as before.

It is known in the village that this practicing magician who also owns magic books with which he carries on black magic, does not only have the ability of magic persecution but also can get money through spiritistic apports. As evidence in this case the certificate of the Animal Biological Institute at Zurich can be shown. Besides two local ministers in whose presence the man made a confession, authenticate this story. The veterinarian admitted during a personal talk, that he had examined the pigs for the cause of death several times but had found nothing. He also suspected magical connections. I got the report from the victimized farmer personally who came to me for Christian counseling.

In the meantime I visited this farmer again. In the presence of the new minister the farmer declared that he had followed the advice I had given him two years ago. His wife as well as he and his whole family have decided to become followers of Jesus. A prayer circle was started which has met faithfully in this house for the last two years. Since that time no more pigs have died. Here Christ has been also victorious over the dark powers.

5. Problems and Explanations

The evaluation of these examples gives an abundance of clues which can only sketchily be pointed out.

a) Psychological aspects: The superstitious and magically working person who believes in his occult practices, succumbs to a fulfilment compulsion. Unconsciously he himself fulfils that which he wants to force through his magical manipulations. He is a victim of an auto-suggestion if one does not want to acknowledge further connections. At the least the occult customs have a corruptible, suggestive character.

b) Parapsychological aspects: The examples also point to an objectively stated fact that with black and white magic, as it is practiced in connection with the 6th and 7th Book of Moses, influences can be exerted on other people which no longer can be explained in a suggestive way. May it be pointed out in this connection that the humbug theory, held by many rationalists, for instance Dr. Gubisch and teacher Kruse, is not tenable according to my knowledge of these things. The problems are not that easy.

c) Psychiatric aspects: In families which experiment with the 6th and 7th Book of Moses, there is an enormous increase of mental illnesses, emotional disturbances and other psychic and nervous disorders. Psychiatrists usually believe that here cause and effect are being mistaken. The cause is supposed to be the sickly psychic constitution of the person, the effect magic experimentation. But in counseling with thousands of occultly working people, the opposite sequence is also shown. In many cases it can be proved that magic was the cause or at least the triggering, decisive factor in psychic disturbances. These facts are also recognized by some believing Christian psychiatrists, for instance Dr. Lechler, the medical superintendent of the health resort 'Hohe Mark'. Prof. Dr. Bender also knows the so-called mediumistic psychosis.

d) Christian-religious aspects: Magic creates a defence against all Biblical things, so-called resistance. This is also true in white magic which is the practice of magic under the cover of religion. Basically magic experimentation and the thus caused occult subjection is a religious phenomenon. Psychological and psychiatric categories do not do justic to this religious aspect. According to the Biblical concept demonic powers stand behind the use of magic no matter if it sails under a black, white or neutral flag. These facts cannot be demonstrated, just as the existence of God or of the devil cannot be demonstrated mathematically. But there are very many characteristics and clues which point to demonic factors in magic.

e) Legal aspects: Many misdemeanours and crimes happen in the area of magic. Often terrible things were revealed to me in confessions. Unfortunately such matters can hardly be dealt with in a legal way since scientific demonstrations fail to prove metaphysical things. One usually has to depend upon frequency relations and drastic clues in connection with magic. The principle of simple causality hardly ever appears in a way that the law can lay hold on it.

f) Mental health aspects: In the interest of the

180

public's mental health, it would be desirable that magic literature would disappear from among the people. But this is almost impossible to accomplish since many farm families have handwritten occult books. Many magic charms are only passed on orally from one generation to the next. In any case a beginning could be made in prohibiting new editions, such as are being printed in Braunschweig and Pfullingen and other places. Furthermore professional groups which especially engage in magic should be better supervised. To this group belong many nature healers, mesmerizers, magnetizers, lay practitioners, clairvoyants, fortune-tellers, pendulum practitioners and others. According to the experiences of well-known Christian counselors, these professional groups work up to 90% in an occult, magic manner. The psychic injury done to the people through magic is immense.

In view of the occult infection of our people and of the European countries with the 6th and 7th Book of Moses, Christian counseling has a twofold task. Pertinent enlightenment and authoritative Christian counseling help and guidance is needed. The time of the Old Testament stonings of the magicians is passed. Also the dark periods of witch burnings have come to a final end. Our task is not to be accomplished through the use of force but the battle for enlightenment has to be waged with spiritual weapons. This watchman office must not be undermined and be made powerless from the beginning through a crying ignorance of magic. Magic connections cannot be grasped with the functions of our five senses because extrasensory, metaphysical and religious facts are underlying here. Next to the warning service the counselor's task is the care of the already subjected person. Because occult subjection is a religious issue, it ought not to be treated by psychiatry and psychotherapy. People who have been occultly subjected have become an object and target of demonic influences. Neither medical men nor theologians can help here but Christ alone. There is only one place where the subjected person can be freed, that is at the cross of Golgotha. The cross is the sign of deliverance and redemption. To the human reason this is a 'scandalon' (offence). The deliverance of subjected people is not a matter of reason but a specifically New Testament event. Faith in Christ stops the demonic power. Christ stands as the light of the world over the darkness of the satanic onslaught. For this purpose the Son of God was manifested that he might destroy the works of the devil. On the cross Christ has conquered the power of darkness.

# E. DIVINE HEALING TODAY

James 5, 14—16

Is any sick among you? let him call for the elders of the church; and let them pray over him, anointing him with oil in the name of the Lord: and the prayer of faith shall save the sick, and the Lord shall raise him up; and if he have committed sins, they shall be forgiven him. Confess your faults one to another, and pray one for another, that ye may be healed.

E 166   A Protestant minister told me, that one day a sick man of his congregation requested that he and the elders should lay hands on him and pray for him. The minister asked different elders but everywhere he was turned down. None had ever done such a thing. Nobody thought that he was capable of doing it. It was an unfamiliar act to all of them.

Why is this Biblical laying on of hands so little known in Christendom? Why do also the Christians who know these references to faith healing, usually not have the courage to apply them? Why does so-called Christendom leave these passages to the sects, the cults or the fanatics? Are these promises of Holy Scripture only for the extremist groups? Does the church of Christ testify to its poverty that it does no longer live in the fulness of the promises of the Bible? These are all questions which are very relevant to our present time. Let us trace these problems with reference to the letter of James.

1. In order not to get on the wrong track from the beginning, as so many sectarian groups do, first we have to examine the religious historical source of the passage in James 5, 14. In the Jewish community it was the custom that the sick requested the elders to come. Special help was expected through their prayer. This fine custom was taken over by the Christian church. Behind this Jewish custom lies the idea that the sick person was a special sinner, a person afflicted by God. Fortunately in the Christian laying on of hands this negative attitude has disappeared. The anointing with oil has to be explained. The Old Testament knows the anointing of priests and kings. Furthermore anointing was an expression of festive joy. We think of Psalm 23: "Thou anointest my head with oil, my cup runneth over." In connection with our text the fact is of great importance that the medical art considered oil as the best healing medicine. This is an indication that in spite of the intercession of the elders, medical help was not rejected. In the time of the Old Covenant, oil was not only a liturgic means but also a medicine. A parallel can be drawn from the use of oil in antiquity to the use of saliva. In ancient times oil and saliva were thought to be precious healing means. Even today this idea can be found occasionally on the mission field. One day a missionary friend was caught in an embarrassing situa-

tion in India. After he had spat on the ground an Indian woman ran after him, returned his saliva and requested him not to throw away his best. We have to keep these religious historical facts in view. The fanatics who think that they have to reject medical help because of this passage in James can be shown that just this passage has a reference to medical help. Of course in the first place this passage is concerned with prayer and faith healing. Nothing should be said against the believing Christian, who thinks he does not have to call a doctor but only has to wait for the help of the Lord. But such attitude of faith should not be made a law to others. I know of many bad experiences in this regard.

The most important religious historical point, which Bible expositors commonly name is the contrast of this passage in James to magic healing as it was practiced in antiquity. In the Ancient World sicknesses were thought to be caused by demons. Healing therefore was equal with excorcising the evil spirits. Healing consisted of calling on the name of the respective spirit by the excorcist, the magic charmer, or in calling on the name of a stronger god. We know of such an act of excorcism in Acts 19, 13—16. Traveling Jews tried to excorcise in the Name of Jesus, without being followers of Jesus themselves. This unsuccessful excorcism cost them dearly. We could now dispose of these magic healings as a surpassed religious historical fact, if these magic healings would not happen even today to a great extent. With this we come to the timely part of our topic.

2. Practically all sick people are contemplating the question: "How will I get well?" This question is justifiable. First the physician is consulted. If medicine does not bring the hoped-for help, then some people turn to occult healings methods. They consult people who have magic powers, who can charm, 'bless' 'atone' 'do something for it'. These magic healings happen in the 20th century in the same way as they have been practiced in antiquity and over thousands of years. The magic healer, the banner of sicknesses, the charmer calls upon the name of a powerful spirit to entreat him to help. In Christian counseling I met with many kinds of such healings. A few of the most important I will briefly sketch here.

a) Easiest to discern are healings in the area of black magic. Here one knows immediately with whom one has to do. An example shall introduce the healing method.

E 167   A woman with psychic disturbances came for Christian counseling. During the conversation an amulet was discovered. At first the woman refused to turn over the amulet because then she would die within three days. Thus the magic charmer had warned her. Finally she handed it over and was shocked, when after opening it, she found a piece of paper with the words: "My soul belongs to the D." It turned out that this woman had had TB and had been healed by a magic charmer who called upon three devils' names. After turning over the amulet, her old disease reappeared. But she found the way to Christ and trustingly put her fate into His hands.

b) Not as simple to be discerned as black magic is white magic. The forms of white magic are found in greater numbers among the people than those of black magic. This has its reason in the fact that white magic is being practiced under religious camouflage. One does not recognize immediately the background as in the case of the black art. The religious trimming is confusing. An example shall show this.

E 168   The doctors in a hospital told a woman that they would have to amputate her diseased leg. The troubled patient wanted to try everything to prevent the amputation and without the doctor's knowledge she asked a charmer to visit her. The magic healer told the patient: "You have to believe in me." Then he spoke his magic charm and prayed three Lord's prayers. Immediately after the charming the pain ceased. The leg did not have to be amputated. This turn of events was a puzzle to the doctors. But from the time of this magic charming the healed woman suffered serious psychic disturbances. Afterwards her family also was afflicted with many accidents.

Healings of white magic take place under religious symbols, like the three highest names, three Lords' prayers, three Scripture verses, three Psalms,

three crosses and so on. Through this naive people
— sometimes also those with a theological education
— are deceived. One believes this healing method to
be Christian. In reality such healing falls under the
Second Commandment: "Thou shalt not take the
name of the Lord thy God in vain. For the Lord will
not hold him guiltless that taketh his name in vain."
Our God cannot be forced by man. He is not our
handy-man who has to obey when the magic charmer commands. The Bible relegates all charms and
all Scripture words that have been turned into
empty formulas into the area of sorcery (Deut. 18,
10—12). Many times white magic is black magic under Christian camouflage. II Cor. 11, 14 is fulfilled
here: "Satan is transformed into an angel of light."
White magic's use of force in prayer is something
totally different from the attitude of faith and
prayer of the Christian: "Lord, Thy will be done."

c) In the same category as the religously camouflaged white magic belongs the professional prayer
of healing. An example to this.

E 169   A businessman with an organic disease
consulted a man who for a good fee would pray for
his health. A few days later the sick man visited
some friends and complained: "I cannot pray any
more. I have the feeling as if dark powers surround
me." Daily he forced himself to read his New Testament. But he could not do it. In his distress he turned again to his friends and asked them: "Help me.
Dark powers, such as I have never known in my

life, are troubling me." This battle lasted for several months. The organic disease had disappeared but instead he was troubled by psychic disturbances and disorders. Finally this strange battle ended in an act of desperation. The businessman, father of four children, took his life. If this would be only an isolated case the evidence would be inconclusive. I have a file of over three thousand such counseling cases which make it possible to judge the magic healing methods.

d) A further healing movement which is difficult to be judged by non-theologians, is being much talked about in the present. Dr. Trampler, who evidently knows Groening's healing method well, experiences astounding healings on his patients almost daily. Even chronic, organic diseases are often healed very quickly. What powers and principles are being used in this new healing movement? This will be discussed here only briefly. This new healer speaks of a plan-animated power which flows through him and then over into his patients. For a better reception of these cosmic powers from the universe, the finger tips can be held up high or aluminium foil be used. It is advised to put aluminium foil under the pillow at night also or to wear it on the body. From the religious point of view many directions meet together in this new healer. He speaks of God and Christ but also acknowledges other great religions as sources of revelation. In reality this could mean for instance: Christ and Buddha and

189

not Christ or Buddha. The clear line of the New Testament is forsaken. The teaching of the new healer is a mixture of pantheistic, mystic, natural-religious and Christian elements. A dangerous, misleading mixture. The difference between this healing movement and vital faith in Christ shall be shown in a counseling example.

E 170   A woman church member traveled to the healer to get help for an organic disease. With many other patients she sat in the waiting room and prayed fervently. The healer came, walked through the rows and talked to each individual. As he stood before the praying woman, he declared tersely: "I cannot help you." Then he proceeded to the next patient.

This experience falls into the pattern of many observations that I could make in connection with magic healings.

e) A spiritistic healing method was reported to me by a student.

E 171   A British lay medical practitioner came to Germany to show off his art here. For a time he also worked in Heidelberg. He declared that a deceased surgeon had appeared unto him from the realm of the dead and had transmitted to him his ability to operate and heal. Since this alleged appearance from the dead he carries out fictitious operations. He is supposed to have had many successful healings. There is never an end to the credulous and superstitious. But with this student the miracle surgeon had no success.

f) Another healing movement in a certain sense is Christian Science. I cannot give a detailed picture of this movement here. Hutten has done this in his book of sects. The founder Mary Baker Eddy, taught that sickness and death are illusions and not reality. Man could overcome the error of disease through the creative, divine spirit that lives in him. The dream of death would be done away with through the mind. Because of this statement by Mother Eddy, her followers then believed that she would not die. Of course this expectation was not fulfilled. The effects that are sometimes seen as a result of the teachings of Christian Science, shall be shown in an example which I experienced myself.

E 172   A young man was in a cast with a fractured leg. A follower of Mother Eddy visited him and declared his fracture was unreal. He should take off the cast, get up and walk home. He did not need to be sick. His sickness was an illusion, an unreal notion. Certainly this was only a primitive follower of Christian Science. But she had hit on an important part of the teaching with this strange advice.

g) The flood of strange healing movements is rising more and more. We live in an era of human history, in which uncontrollable forces and demonic powers are on the increase. One sensation chases the other.

191

E 173   It is being reported from Syracuse, Italy, that a wooden picture cries tears that have healing power. I traveled to Sicily and saw the healing and crying Madonna in Syracuse. Every three months tears come from the wooden picture. On these days about 50 people get well. Over 800 have already been counted as healed.

E 174   In America the late sect leader Father Divine gave himself out as God and his son as Christ. Both men were supposed to have the ability of healing and killing at distance. A foreign evangelist who was my guest, declared that his mother had been killed by this sect leader who works with black magic.

E 175   From the Near East comes the report that Prince Abdul, a relative of ex-King Farouk, can perform great miracles. He let fire fall from heaven as Elijah had done and imitated the New Testament miracles of Jesus. He is also supposed to heal the sick and resurrect the dead like Christ.

E 176   In South France George de Montfavet also gives himself out as the returned Christ. Several hundred miracles, which are reported of him shall be evidence of his claim. Mankind tumbles today from one sensational news to another. A scintillating line of miracle workers, healers, saviors and helpers dance before our eyes. Who can still see clearly?

h) This question of intellectual and spiritual perception is especially important at the dividing line between magic and divine miracles. There are also miracle healers of which a judgment is extremely difficult. At the present time there is Tommy Hicks, Oral Roberts, Osborn and Branham. All have in common religious mass meetings followed by healing meetings. What I have to say about these men is no superficial judgment of spiteful criticism. For many years I have carefully collected every available material about these miracle healers, read all favourable or unfavourable publications, heard them personally, examined their healings, and compared everything with the Holy Scripture. I am concerned about observing the Word of the Bible: "Prove the spirits, whether they are of God." It is impossible to unfold all of the material in this sketch. Only a few points will be discussed.

Without doubt Branham is the most problematic of these men. He exhibits fortune-telling, animal-magnetic, mesmerizing, magical but also Biblical attributes. Everything is covered over with Christian words. From his parents who believed and listened to fortune-tellers he received certain occult subjections. In Karlsruhe he declared: "From birth on I had a visionary disposition." I myself was a witness to this statement. Here a Biblical fact is being disregarded. The gifts of the Spirit (charismata) are not imparted at natural birth but at the spiritual rebirth.

E 177 The following typical case happened in Zurich. Branham called a young man to the platform. The following conversation took place: "We don't know each other." "No", said the young man. "You are carrying in your suit pocket the letter of a young lady." "Yes." "In the letter is a picture of me." "That's right." "Show the picture." The young man pulled it out. Then Branham lifted up the photo and turned to the audience with the question: "Am I not a prophet of God?" Enthusiastic 'Hallelujah' shouting is the answer.

We ask: Shall a fortune-teller trick be prophetic evidence? Here fortune-telling is mistaken for prophecy. The powers of fortune-telling come from below (Acts 16, 16). Prophecy comes from the inspiration of the Holy Spirit (Acts 21, 11). Why is Branham so anxious to give evidences of his prophetship? What about the fetishistic (pagan, objective, magic) custom to bless a box full of paper napkins and to pass them out among the sick? This has really nothing to do with Acts 19, 12. Why is Branham so exhausted after his lectures like a pumped out mesmerizer? Jesus and his disciples were not led away staggering and completely exhausted when people were healed in the authority of God. — Why is Branham being disturbed in his healing activity through praying brothers who sit in the audience? Twice he declared in such cases: "There are counter-currents". Branham did not know that we had scattered a group of praying people among the audience, who were calling upon the Lord for clear understanding. Immediately Branham was hindered from doing anything. Therefore he acted like the occult lay practitioner who had a praying person sitting in his waiting room. There are so many evidences — they cannot all be named here — which lead to the following possible conclusion: Branham is occultly subjected. He has mediumistic abilities. In his youth he came to Christ, and unconsciously dragged these dark abilities into the discipleship of Jesus. Today he as well as his followers, mistake these abilities for gifts of the Spirit. The effects of his ministry are dividing and confusing Christian circles. He is the definite type of fanatic of whom the Scripture-bound Christian has to warn. It is significant also that American men of God, like Billy Graham, disassociate themselves from Branham and his movement. While Branham works on a mediumistic basis in Christian attire, there are in the case of Hicks next to the Christian elements also strong suggestive abilities. His healings often occur on the level of psychic shock effects. An example:

E 178   A university graduate with education in psychology suffered from chronic paralysis. After a treatment by Hicks the paralysis regressed. During the following three weeks the old sickness returned progressively. The patient himself defined the passing improvement as effects of suggestive shock therapy. Just as in the case of Branham, suggestions (psychic influences) by Hicks are mistaken for gifts of the Spirit because they are used together with Christian words and prayers.

13   *

3. We have now made a little survey over the different healing movements of the present, beginning with healings through the black art, followed by reports of so-called neutral healing methods and ending with healing movements on the fringe of the Christian realm. What can be said about these healing movements from the Word of God, specially in view of the passage in James 5, 14? In many ways these healing movements are a Biblical symptom.

a) We live in a time in which the mystery of iniquity doth already work (II Thess. 2, 7). Jesus has predicted that false Christs shall rise, who will do demonic signs and wonders (Mark 13, 22) and many will be seduced by these. The effect of this seduction becomes alarmingly clear in the fact that many of our Christian circle do not see through the occult healing methods. They are taken in by every religiously camouflaged act.

b) These healing movements are also a sign that the Christian church has failed in one area. The point of interest has shifted from dealing with spiritual problems to dealing with material, physical problems. The difficulty in the Christian church is their lack of faith in the reliability of the promises of Holy Scripture. Counseling was handled one-sidedly in an unhealthy manner. The Word of God gives effective help to those who dare stand on the promises.

c) James has a decisive word to say about the question of healing. Healing stands in healthy connection with confession and forgiveness of sin. In the New Testament healing and forgiveness are not to be divided. The order of precedence is such that forgiveness, the healing of the inner man, is placed above outward healing. This is best shown in the example of the lame man. One gets on the wrong track when both healing processes are being divided or given wrong precedence. Magic healing is concerned only in outward healing. Here the motto is: "If it only helps, no matter how." In the Holy Scriptures the first concern is inner healing which can, but not necessarily has to be followed by outward healing. Sometimes the Lord allows His child to suffer in order to excercise his faith and patience in the maturing process for eternity. An example of healing shall be reported which happened in the Biblical frame-work.

E 179    A young woman suffered from a throat infection in connection with a tumor, the size of an egg. The treatment by physician and neurologist was unsuccessful. Then she came for Christian counseling and confessed that she had committed a serious wrong in the absence of her husband. By faith she received assurance of forgiveness of her sins and found peace with God. After a few weeks the POW husband returned. Without a special invitation she returned once more with her husband for counseling, and voluntarily repeated her confession. — She had not been advised to do so. — The husband forgave her. After three days the throat infection and the tumor had disappeared. Inner healing had been followed by outer healing.

With Jesus and His disciples this natural, Biblical healing process belonged to the basic elements of the kingdom of God. Therefore all of those who have experienced a spiritual resurrection with Christ and who live the abiding life, may act on the word in James 5, 14 and Mark 16, 17: "And these signs shall follow them that believe: In my name shall they lay hands on the sick, and they shall recover." The thousandfold misuse of magic healings must not darken or rob us of the New Testament order of Christian counseling and the Biblical laying on of hands in faith. Where the sin of dark magic procedure aboundeth, there the grace of Christ does much more abound.

In conclusion the two basic forms of healing shall be lined up once more. The Bible knows about magic help. We only have to think of the Egyptian magicians, the Canaanite conjurers or Simon Magus. Magic help brings relief in the organic sphere. But here the short-circuit happens: Help shall be given to the body, but the psychic connections and the ensuing disturbances are disregarded. This method is obviously a defection from the arch-order of the Scriptures: More important than all physical relationships is man's personal relationship to God. In magic the question is: "What helps?" In the New Testament the question is: "Who helps?" The magic practitioner says: "It helps." The Christian declares:

"He helps." Behind the "What" and "It" of magic is the twilight of uncontrollable powers and forces. Somebody is hiding there. Behind the "Who" and "He" of the Christian faith stands the living Lord. "The Lord shall raise him up" testifies James in gratitude and joyous trust. This same Lord works yesterday, today and in all eternity. Out of thankfulness should we not give our whole life to this Lord, Jesus Christ?

# F. REPORTS OF BIBLICAL HEALINGS
## AND DELIVERANCES

## 1. CHRIST, THE VICTOR OVER DARK POWERS

It was in the year 1935, when I served in an evangelization in M. (Haut Rhin). After the meeting a couple and their 15 year old son introduced themselves. They told me the following story: Their farm is located in the high Vosges Mountains. For a few decades already curious things were happening in their house. The husband stated that strange spooks had been observed in the house. He himself had been plagued much from childhood on. Besides he had strange symptoms of paralysis. The physician could not explain this sickness. Also the cattle in the stables were troubled. The cows were fearful and acted wildly. When the stable was examined they stood together in a group perspiringly. They also showed evidences of paralysis. The man's parents had to sell seven cows in one year. Since only one cow was left, they faced financial ruin. Then the old farmer heard about a man who could help in such cases. This man had the reputation of being a master of witchcraft. The farmer asked the man to come and he began strange ceremonies in the stables. In the ensuing time peace returned. The number of cattle increased again.

In the meantime the First World War had started. The sorcerer had to go to war. Because this particular area of the Vosges Mountains was turned into a theater of war the farmers were forced to give up their home. For four years they lived as refugees in the interior of the country. After the war the farmer's son married. While he had felt quite well during his time in the service, now disturbing symptoms appeared again. After the birth of their first child the infant suffered from strange attacks and could not sleep. A magic charmer was called who helped the infant. A second child was born which was also plagued. At the age of six weeks this infant died after a terrible three hour long death struggle.

After the death of this boy, the father was again plagued and suffered from abnormal physical symptoms. After prolonged medical treatment and weeks of observation in a hospital, he had to return home without the slightest improvement. There he was plagued day and night so that he grew emaciated like a sceleton. Every time he tried to fall asleep he was startled by terrible buffetings and sometimes he was lifted up as if by invisible hands and then again thrown down. The house was filled with knocking, scratching and shuffling noises. At times one heard the sound of doors closing. To top it off the whole house was filled with a nauseous smell.

When the man tried to take refuge in prayer, he was shaken terribly by an unseen power. Once, though he was extremely weak, he was desperate enough to leave his bed. He took an old prayer book and sat at the table to pray and to call upon God in his distress. Suddenly he felt a terrible pressure around his loins. As if grabbed by powerful hands, he felt himself being lifted up and then thrown down upon his chair with such force that he thought he would burst.

Finally another man was called in for help who was supposed to be able to do something. After his advice had been followed, these conditions slowly came to an end. But some time later strange things began to happen in the stables again. The cattle was plagued and the fields and garden did not grow. Later the oldest son also fell victim to these strange attacks. As mentioned earlier his son had been freed once from similar attacks by a charmer when he was an infant.

Now the man no longer trusted the charmers and lay practitioners. He consulted several physicians for the treatment of his boy but no definite improvement could be seen. In his fifteenth year the boy experienced terrible things. He was almost plagued to death and saw monstrous figures walk around the house. One morning while getting up he was grabbed on his arms by powerful hands, which resulted in a total paralysis of his right arm. In spite of a long treatment and observation in the hospital no improvement was shown.

As these people stood before me with their son after that evangelistic meeting, I observed that the son's right arm hung totally lame and limp by his side. I addressed a few questions to the parents and recognized by their statements the background behind all of these tragic events. Then I told the people about the terrible consequences of sins of magic and challenged them to repent and turn to God with their whole heart. By using several Scripture passages I made it clear to them that in such cases physicians could not help but Jesus Christ alone Who has come to destroy the works of Satan. Afterwards the parents confessed their sin and declared that they wanted to follow the Lord Jesus. The son also was willing to follow Jesus. I prayed over him in the Name of Jesus. In His grace the Lord answered the prayer and healed the young man. A few days later he helped his father with mowing. From now on the peace of God rested upon the house. The Lord's blessing was on the stables and fields. —

During the Second World War, when Strassbourg was evacuated I found shelter with my family as refugees in this farm in the Vosges Mountains. The Lord Jesus Christ has glorified Himself in this whole family. Since then family, house and home are filled with the spirit of peace.

Henri Waechter, Evangelist in Strassbourg.


## 2. THE BULWARKS OF DARKNESS

It was in the year 1938. I held an evangelization in Hesse. One special counseling session will remain unforgettable. A young man in his twenties appeared and told about his troubles. His emotional disorder was so typical that I told him right away, that he had engaged in occult things, or that such things had been practiced in his family. He frankly admitted it. What he told me then was so terrible, that it impressed itself deeply upon my mind. If I tell about it here I do not violate the seal of confession, because the young man requested me to warn of this terrible field whereever I could, based on his experience. In fact he gave permission to use his name and fate as deterrent. But that is not necessary.

Let us begin with this young man. From childhood on he suffered from depressions, thoughts of suicide and psychic disorders. At night he was often startled by strange knocking signs from an unexplainable source. Or he would be frightened by whizzing and rustling noises made by strange appearances. The psychiatrist would perhaps diagnose these abnormal manifestations as psychoneurosis, without getting to the cause of these psychic disturbances through this. The story of the family history made all connections clear.

The great-grandmother of the young man was a magic charmer. She healed animals and people in her strange manner. Beside these demonic healing methods she also belonged to a spiritistic circle which practiced intercourse with the departed spirits. The terrible tragedy of this family began with this woman who deeply engaged in occult things.

The son and daughter of this woman continued in the tradition of the mother. Both charmed people and animals with the help of the 6th and 7th Book of Moses and carried on relations with the dead. They also were pendulum practitioners with song books and keys and layed cards for fortune-telling purposes. They both had a terrible end. At night the woman saw spooks in her room. She had the feeling as if evil spirits held her mouth and nose shut. This went on for years till the woman was committed to an insane asylum. Since she was not mentally ill, she was released again after half a year. The brother of this woman died in terrible agony. Before his death he begged his relatives to burn all magic books or throw them out of the house. He asked for the Bible but could no longer understand anything. Under terrible pain and by spreading an obnoxious stench he entered eternity.

In the line of the grandchildren it did not look any better. One granddaughter often had attacks of frenzy during which she broke her furniture to pieces. Sometimes she laid down in the street and screamed with superhuman strength. She carried on this way till she was committed to an insane asylum. A second granddaughter heard at night the already mentioned knocking signs. She was so disturbed emotionally that one day she killed herself and her two children, ages five and eight by jumping off a 120 foot high cliff. A grandson was used as medium in spiritistic séances. He suffered from persecution mania, and like the other members of his clan, he ended in an insane asylum.

In the line of the great-grandchildren there was a girl who continued in the card laying and charming tradition. She died early. Her brothers and sisters assert that she haunts the house as a restless spirit, a poltergeist. The brother of this girl is the young man who reported this family history. He confessed to me that he had suffered so unspeakably under all these things that he strongly warns everybody from engaging in occult things. For all these terrible psychic disorders he only makes magic responsible, in which all of these family members engaged through the generations. Here again the judgment of the First Commandment becomes evident: "... visiting the iniquity of the fathers upon the children unto the third and fourth generation of them that hate me." — This is not only an isolated case which I report here. In my ministry in National Missions I have heard many such family histories in counseling sessions. It is distressing that in psychiatry and Christian counseling the demonic power of magic is too little known and underestimated. It is a result of rationalism that such things are made light of or are represented as humbug. If we want to give such bound people counseling help then we have to take the satanic influences in the lives of people seriously. Man stands in the heat of the battle b e t w e e n C h r i s t a n d S a t a n. Where Satan is only represented as a scarecrow or laughing-stock for tomfoolery and masquerade, a terribly rele-vant reality is passed by, and Satan can ensnare and tear down his victims unhinderedly. The most dan-gerous area of satanic seduction is magic; for there satanic help is being applied consciously even if this help is camouflaged by pious ceremonies.

Thank God the demonic power on this earth is not the last that can be said to people. Jesus Christ has come to destroy the works of the devil (1 John 3, 8). We have a mighty enemy but an almighty friend, as the late German evangelist, Ernst Moder-sohn, used to say. The right hand of the Lord doeth valiantly, also with people who have been driven into direct demonic dependence through occupation with occult things. This was also shown in the life of the young man about whom I reported here. Christ gave him joy and freedom. The chains and fetters broke under the almighty hand of the great victor of Golgotha. Jesus Christ is and remains victor for all eternity.

## 3. THE WORKS OF THE DEVIL

A physically robust and mentally healthy woman had increasingly strange experiences at night. She had the feeling as if she was being beaten although she observed no one in the room. In the morning she had black and blue marks on her body. This was repeated once or twice a week. She did not know how to explain these puzzling events. At first she was ashamed to talk about it because she did not want to become the talk of the people. Finally in her distress she sought counseling help. She asked the local minister for advice. He did not know what to make of these happenings. The woman did not at all give the impression of being a neurotic or mentally disturbed person. She was completely normal in other areas of her life. Another minister who was consulted, also had no knowledge about this strange field and could not help the woman.

One day a friend of mine who knows about the occult field through his work, visited the woman. Since this was not a case of emotional or mental disturbance, he inquired about the field of magic. After talking the matter out fully, the following story came to light. During her youth the woman had been courted by a young man, who had wanted to marry her under any condition. Since the passionate suitor impressed her as being an obscurantist, the girl rejected him. Thereupon the man threatened her: "I'll plague you." At first the girl did not think about this threat. She was not afraid and paid no attention to the talk. Only after she experienced the nightly disturbances and the black and blue marks became visible before everybody's eyes, she was reminded of this. But she still could not believe that such a thing was possible.

Before we continue with this story, let me briefly point out, how I deal with such cases. If such people come to me I first examine whether there are any medical, psychiatric causes behind these experiences. If this can be found, then I send the patient to a believing Christian psychiatrist. Often puzzling occurrences can also be understood through the recent findings of depth psychology. In judging these cases, extreme caution and restraint is necessary. A wrong diagnosis can have disastrous effects. If all scientific border areas have been consulted then the findings of parapsychology or occultism can be applied, if such connections can be shown. And there is much more here than our medical men, psychologists and theologians know through university education. Occult practices are found among the people in tremendous numbers.

Let us return to our case. My friend interceded fervently for the troubled woman. He pointed out to her that she must commit herself completely to Christ if she wanted to be freed. Only in Christ there is complete deliverance in this area. After this advice and the ensuing counseling battle a strange thing happened. The man who had threatened to plague her hanged himself. From that day on the woman was free. The experiences never recurred.

This case belongs to the controversial field of mental suggestion at a distance. Even if our modern rationalists declare these things to be humbug and deception, this field is not understood in its terrible reality by this explanation. Schopenhauer said: "There is also a scepticism of ignorance." Here also Shakespeare's words apply that there are still things between heaven and earth which this world has never dreamed of. The field of mental suggestion has been examined by quite a few doctors. I only mention Drs. Dusart, Janet and Gibert, who could influence their subjects at a distance of 10 km. In Christian counseling, these phenomena are found especially in connection with the dangerous magic book, the 6th and 7th Book of Moses. Enough cases of mental suggestion are known to me which are strong evidence that they cannot be done away with simply as a popular superstition.

Even if in our case these nightly disturbances would have been symptoms of hysteria or another thymopathy, sudden and lasting healing would be an extraordinary thing in any case. Every physician knows how difficult it is to heal such sicknesses. But in this situation it was not such a sickness but magic influence. For the Christian it is an open secret that man is surrounded and enclosed by demonic and satanic powers. Christ did not have to come if the idea of the devil would have been only a delusion of an unenlightened time. No, the power of darkness is a reality but a reality which has been overcome by Christ. Therefore the Son of God came to destroy the works of the devil. He is the victor over all dark forces.

# 4. INCURABLY INSANE

A believing Christian told me the story of his ancestors and of his own family. The great-grand-parents carried on magic practices. As results of these occult activities, there were mediumistic faculties in the line of the grandparents. The grand-mother had psychic disturbances. She suffered from depressions and had an irascible, selfish disposition. The psychic disturbances grew worse till they led to attacks of frenzy. She had to be tied and in this condition was committed to a mental hospital. In the third generation who are the parents of my reporter, again psychic disturbances like depressions, hallucinations and neurotically caused functional organic disorders were observed. When the father accepted Christ he was freed from all symptoms of compulsion and psychic complications. Our reporter stands now in the fourth generation of this family. In his youth he had to fight much against depressions but Christ completely delivered him. In the fifth generation stands this man's son, about whom a detailed account shall be given.

According to his father this young man had been a friendly and good-natured child. When he was 18 years old, like his ancestors, he developed an emotional and later mental illness. At first he had depressions, which were coupled with a strong fear of life. The depressive period then was succeeded by varied obsessions. He would kneel and pray for hours. Then again he had fits of frenzy and beat his parents. After these attacks he ran off into the woods where he roamed for days till he collapsed from exhaustion. Forestry workers usually brought the unfortunate man home. He was fired from his job because of this condition. As a further step schizophrenic symptoms appeared. He heard knocking signs in the house, saw lights and heard voices, which challenged him not to obey his parents any longer but only to follow his inner voice. Under these circumstances the parents felt compelled to have their son examined by a psychiatrist. This psychiatrist gave the following diagnosis: Incurable high grade schizophrenia, to be committed to an insane asylum.

The father refused to have his son committed. He started a small prayer circle with believers and together they interceded for the seriously ill young man. Then he took his son to a Christian convalescent home, which was directed by a well-known man of God. The mentally-ill man continued his fugues in this home. Every day the director of the home sat together with the young man, read a few encouraging Bible verses to him and prayed with him. At first this counseling treatment had a negative effect. The patient was plagued by religious delusions. In public he knelt by a bench and prayed for hours. This spectacle often repeated itself. Then the director of the home started a prayer circle which also interceded for the sick man. After a few weeks there was a perceptible improvement in his condition. At the end of the sixth week, during a counseling session, suddenly the mind of the young man became completely clear. His impulsions and compulsions stopped completely. After two weeks of observation the director of the home could send his patient home as cured. The young man could once again return to his profession. Today he is the chief construction engineer of a large company and he has proved himself as a vital Christian. For eighteen years there have been no signs of the former mental illness. The incurable, high grade schizophrenia as it was diagnosed by the psychiatrist had been healed by Christ.

Two lines can be seen throughout this whole family history. The ancestors engaged in magic and occult practices. Emotional and mental illnesses appeared in the descendants through four generations. In three generations, grandfather, father and son, these psychic disturbances disappeared when they turned to Christ. This report shows that the power of Jesus Christ can yet perform miracles, where the medical art has come to an end. With God there are no hopeless cases. Through faith creative and renewing forces are unfolding in the life of the follower of Jesus. Once a doctor who worked much with Christians, stated: "With Christians one must be very careful of the diagnosis. If today they are lying on their death-bed they can meet you at the door tomorrow, happy and healthy.

Their faith is so unpredictable, that they often over-
throw the whole medical concept. You never know
where you are with such people."

## 5. REMEMBER NOT THE SINS OF MY YOUTH

A young Swiss who has been a faithful follower
of Jesus for several years, gave me the story of
how he found Jesus. He wrote:

When I was fifteen years old I was charmed
magically because I had some warts on my right
hand. In our locality it was the custom when sickness of any kind appeared not to turn to the physician but to the magic charmer. The charming was
immediately successful. I was freed of the ugly
things but in doing so I came under the influence
of the evil one, under the ban of magic. For years
I fought against the ensuing effects. I began to read
cheap literature. Good books were too boring to me.
Bad movies, with their sultry, sexy atmosphere
fascinated me. All warnings were to no avail. I
became a real addict in this field. I constantly lived
in a sexually disturbed atmosphere. I rebelled
against all divine things. My mind was poisoned by
all the bad things. Sensuality had been awakened
and was giving me much trouble. The compulsion
was so great that I could not get away from certain
things. Again and again I fell. Because of the frequent defeats I was disgusted, irritated and discou-
raged. With this desperate mood and my disobe-

dience I gave my parents and superiors much trouble. Because of this inwardly torn condition I could not concentrate on my job and my work was very unsatisfactory. Therefore I had many failures.

For years I was a victim of my passions and suffered from this subjection. Then the longing for a pure life awakened within me. One day I was invited to a men's meeting. A minister spoke about those things that gave me so much trouble. He pointed out the way to liberation and challenged the men to a decision for Christ. That evening I was hit in my innermost heart but I did not dare to speak to the minister. A false sense of shame hindered me from seeking counsel. I searched for other ways. Finally I thought that I could get rid of all those things which bound me in marriage. I married a woman with three children. Instead of solutions there were new entanglements. I grew more and more miserable. Everything was distasteful and disgusting to me. Where should this all end? God knew a way.

My wife got sick. Then I also was confined to bed. A strange neurosis which the doctors could not diagnose correctly, almost made me despair. A terrible fear that I might never get well again, took hold of me. This was the time when I started to pray fervently. Again and again I called to the Lord for forgiveness and deliverance. Finally it became completely clear to me that I could never deal with these troubles alone. My whole weakness was revealed to me. At that time I received a tract from a friend which showed me the way back. Just at the right moment of my life when I had arrived at the lowest point of my inner need this guidance was given to me. I felt that God is a better psychologist than our doctors and ministers. He knows the time, the kind of help and He can send the right person along. To this friend I opened my heart and confessed all the dark things that were in my life. This was the turning point of my life.

A great joy had come into my life, joy about forgiveness of all sin, joy about the gift of redemption. Through the grace of God it had become also my experience: "If the Son therefore shall make you free, ye shall be free indeed." The prayer of the Psalmist: "Remember not the sins of my youth" had been answered in my life. Forgiveness and redemption had become mine. During my youth I had once learned the verse: "In whom we have redemption through his blood, the forgiveness of sins, according to the riches of his grace", Eph. 1, 7. I had this verse in my mind but I had not experienced it. But now this assurance had been given to me through the Holy Spirit and all the world could have talked against it and still could not have taken it away from me. After all these years of terrible inner misery I had never thought that I could become a joyful person. Through the mercy of God I now know something of His promise: "I am come that they might have life, and have it more abundantly."

# 6. JESUS REDEEMS

Years ago I belonged to the kind of people who, for every case of sickness in the family, sought the help of lay medical practitioners, mesmerizers, nature healers etc. All these men were supposed to be masters of physiotherapy and practiced their uncontrollable healing art with old proven recipes, medicinal herbs and salves. Such medical practitioners were also supposed to develop metaphysical, biological or suggestive treatments. The more high-sounding their name was, the more they could convert their dark art into cash; for they all grew prosperous. In reality almost all of them practiced magic arts in many variations. Mainly magic charming was used. What they all had in common and still have today, is the fact, that they hide their dangerous methods under Christian trimmings. They play the role of the man of honour and also want to appear as Christians. Sometimes they have this reputation. But one who has been initiated into their craft, as it is the case with me, knows that almost all of them have their plug-box at the bottom. They do not draw their powers and gifts from God, neither from a neutral sphere of nature, as they try to make the dumb and naive believe, but from the demonic sphere of power. Long enough I had time to investigate and know about these facts.

For thirty years my father had already practiced this magic healing art. He used his powers of charming on humans and animals with best results. People came from everywhere seeking help and he treated them. Often only a patient's letter or phone conversation with my father was sufficient. Through suggestion healing set in with the patient. Even today this form of healing by telephone is being practiced by hundreds and thousands. Not only simple suggestive or hypnotic effects transmitted at a distance are involved but also magic and demonic powers. The terrible results of my father's charming practice were clearly evident in the whole family and descendants. In spite of this fact, after his death I could not be stopped from learning this magic healing art. The fascination of the unknown and the prospect of effects by forces that are not accessible to everybody, enticed me. I also wanted to master the art in order to have power over human beings and animals. Normally it is not easy to learn this art like a profession but since I was already mediumistically disposed and subjected in this direction through my father, I was successful in getting on in this harmful art. My first healing experiments with members of my own family were successful. Encouraged by this I continued this healing method in my circle of relatives and acquaintances. I was filled with a certain pride that the charming actually worked.

Like my father and my relatives I did not escape the terrible consequences. Quite unexpectedly I had a nervous breakdown. I was so weak and enervated that I had to give up my work. For weeks I sat at home idly and then in the hospital. This was the time when God spoke to me. In the quiet I thought over my life. A further great help was a patient at a health resort in our area who spent his vacation there and started talking to me. I found out that the stranger knew much about the magic charming practice. So we had enough material for conversation. This man warned me of my magic healing method and its effects. He asked a few questions regarding my background. I had to confess that the typical effects of charming were visible in our family. Neither in my parent's nor in my own home was peace. A morose disposition, quarreling, outbursts of temper were the routine of the day. In spite of this fact I did not give in yet. In my defence I said I wanted to help my fellow men with this magic charming and that I would do this through faith in God. The stranger then explained the following: "Through the use of the Holy Name of God, you blaspheme God; for through this misuse you degrade Him to your servant. Because you do this, the devil helps and deceives you; for he is glad when the name of God is misused. You also load upon yourself the sins of your patients. You and your children will be very unhappy through this charming."

At first I rejected such arguments. I did not believe such a thing. But strange enough I could not forget this warning. As I found out afterwards the stranger was praying for me. A terrible battle began in my heart. It went on for weeks. My wife was drawn into this struggle between light and darkness. Finally I was ready to give up magic. But this was easier said than done. I wanted to let go but the powers behind magic did not want to let me go. Then I discovered, that I did not rule these powers but that these powers ruled me. At that moment when I recognized that I was a prisoner, my defence grew so much the more passionate and determined. This was a battle for life or death. My wife became a precious confederate in this. Together we sought help from God, began to read the Bible and prayed also with our children. And still we would have never made it by ourselves. We felt that we were carried through by the mercy of God. A serious operation became a decisive experience. My heart had been under a strain because of these battles. In the hospital the surgeon had to wait for 24 days before he dared to operate. The operation was a success. I was wonderfully carried through and given back to my family. This experience filled us with great joy and thankfulness.

Another foothold in the battle for liberation had been won. But actually I was not completely free yet. While reading the Bible one day I happened to come across a passage in Acts 19, 19: "Many of them also which used curious arts brought their books together, and burned them before all men." Now I began to see my way. I had to get rid of all

of my occult literature. I brought everything together and threw it into the fire. All carefully guarded
treasures, like fast-acting charming formulas and
special recipes went to their just end. These house
idols and magic power centres were dethroned and
removed. With God's help another step to freedom
and relief had been taken.

But the battle still was not finished. Magic always
pulls a long dragon tail of bonds behind it. All black
artists display the effects of magic. So it was also in
my case. In my life there were many open and secret
passions, such as a bad temper, swearing, selfishness,
card playing, alcohol, smoking and other things,
which cannot be told publicly. The longer Christ
had the upper hand in my life, the more I grew
disgusted about all these ties. At the same time my
wife experienced a similar development. For years
she had been plagued by depressions which always
appear in active charmer families and their descendants. Through Christ and the great joy that had
come into our life these depressions disappeared
completely without any medical treatment. This
does not mean that all depressions begin in this
way. There are psychic conditions which develop
from a disease. My wife and I experienced that
Christ can make us free from the worst ties. We
have experienced the truth of Luke 19, 10: "The
Son of Man is come to seek and to save that which
was lost."

The deliverance showed its effects in my life. I

thought that if the Lord Jesus could have helped such a poor sinner as I in soul and body, then He can and will deliver others who are bound in like manner. Therefore it became my mission to help those who have actively or passively engaged in magic and all other arts of sorcery. I began a Gospel ministry against the problems of superstition. The extensive Christian counseling that grew out of it shows how deeply modern man is entangled in these things in spite of all the enlightenment. In spite of the terrible ties in this field, there are no hopeless cases. The Word is true: "Where sin aboundeth, grace does much more abound." The final victory belongs to our Lord Jesus Christ.

H. Buechler

## 7. DELIVERED FROM THE POWER
## OF DARKNESS

During an evangelization I heard the story of an alcoholic. With special permission I want to repeat it here. From his youth he had been a bully and a regular drunkard. Fifteen liters of wine was his daily consumption. Only a few days of the year was he sober. If he did not have enough to drink he ran around like a wounded animal. The smallest occasion was enough for an outburst of temper during which he broke everything to pieces. He had another weakness: girls. None of them were safe from him.

Some were also willing, because in spite of his drinking he was a healty, robust man. He did not want to know anything about God's Word. To believe in God was as much humbug to him as to believe that there was a devil. He had only biting scorn for all Biblical truths. Swearing and cursing had become his second nature when he was with his comrades. One day this was his doom.

In the inn a man spoke of black magic and the possibility of joining up with the underworld. A lot of scary and frightening things were told. A few of the young men laughed and rejected it as silly superstition. Our drunkard was the loudest one and he boasted that he was not afraid to meet the devil and deal with him. With great hullaballoo his drinking companions agreed with him. A bet for 20 DM was made. Jochen, the drunkard would present himself to the devil on Friday midnight at a crossroad outside the village. As a further condition he had to draw a circle around himself with chalk and then call upon Lucifer three times. One of his companions gave him the calling charm to Lucifer. Jochen agreed to these conditions. His comrades accompanied him part of the way and then left him alone. Jochen followed the directions, drew the circle and said the calling charm three times. Expectantly he waited for a reaction. Nothing happened. Triumphantly he returned to his comrades and collected his bet.

However his joy was too soon. As he went to bed

the following night he suddenly saw a horrible face
on the opposite wall of the bed approaching him
slowly. He laid there as if paralyzed and could
not move a finger. The face came closer till it was
about 8 inches away from him. He was terrified.
Finally the face retreated again. Only now could
he scream. His brother-in-law and sister who lived
upstairs rushed down after hearing his murderous
screams. They got as far as the door of the room but
could not enter. They stood banned before the
threshhold. This scene with the face repeated itself
often but only while he was sober. The family members always told him that they could not enter the
room, an unexplainable power would hold them
back. Finally these spook phenomena were too much
for Jochen. He consulted a doctor to find out
whether he had reached the stage of delirium tremens or if alcoholic hallucinosis was setting in. The
doctor examined him thoroughly and denied both
possibilities. He confirmed that he had a strong
heart and robust constitution. As the drunkard
then told him in detail about his experiences with
the devilish face, the doctor grew thoughtful.
He did not dispose of these apparitions as humbug
or overstrained nerves but as a Christian he took
them seriously. He told him: "If you have done such
a thing, it is time that you came to Christ or otherwise the devil will certainly get you." Since the
doctor and the drunkard knew each other from
military service, he told him: "That means: Right

about turn, if you don't want to ruin yourself." What Jochen would not have taken from any minister he took from the doctor. He began to seek Christ in earnest. The appearances of the devil's face had given him such a shock that he could rest neither day nor night. He knelt and cried to God for deliverance from alcohol, from his immoral life, from his bad temper and for deliverance from the claws of Satan. As radical as he had been in sinning, so he was now in committing his life to Christ. He went through days of deepest repentance and inner despair. But it was a confident kind of despair. Christ received him. He experienced complete deliverance. From that moment on the devil's face apparition ceased completely. For Jochen this was a confirmation that these apparitions had not been signs of beginning delirium tremens. They had been the effects of his nightly calling upon Lucifer. Through Jesus Christ the life of the former alcoholic was made completely new. From that time on there was no more alcohol in his life. Twelve years have passed since. To the people around him he has become a living witness to the liberating power of Christ. He works actively in his church and rescue missions. He was elected to the board of directors of his church. Sin had led him to the edge of hell. The power of Christ however had snatched him from Satan's dominion. Since that time the song of praise of the early church rings in Jochen's heart: "Giving thanks unto the Father, which hath made us meet to be partakers of the inheritance of the saints in light who hath delivered us from the power of darkness, and hath translated us into the kingdom of his dear Son." (Col. 1, 12—13).

## 8. BATTLE WITH A POSSESSED WOMAN

One of my Swiss friends told me of his most difficult counseling experience. It concerns counseling and care of his sister-in-law. To understand this case better we will approach it systematically.

Condition of the patient: For many years she suffered from depressions, doubts, difficulties in believing. When she met with Biblical things — whether it was the Word of God, the church, Christian pictures — she displayed violent opposition. At any attempt of giving her religious encouragement she immediately got angry and upset. Psychologists would say, that she had an anti-religious complex caused by religious overfeeding during childhood or by anti-Christian education. Overfeeding was not the cause; for the mother even wanted to know less of Biblical things than her daughter. The daughter showed the often observable characteristic of the demoniac, a violent antipathy against divine things on one hand, and on the other a drive and longing to come to Christ. The psychiatrist would call it split personality. Further it should be noted that the patient often observed spook phenomena in her room as a child. When she screamed for fear she was beaten by these spooks.

Occult previous history of the patient: In reply to questions the woman admitted that she often resorted to fortune-tellers. Her mother also laid cards. In the course of the counseling a decisive factor came to light which shall be mentioned here already. Her mother had promised and subscribed the still unborn child to the devil. At the onset of counseling this fact was not as yet known.

Treatment up to then: For a time members of a fanatical sect had taken care of the patient. She had been prayed for under laying on of hands. Afterwards she was worse than before. After this bad experience she stayed away from the religious, as she expressed it. Then she had been treated by several neurologists. She had also been in a mental hospital for a short time. The repeated diagnosis by the experts is important. She was told again and again: "You are normal mentally, but you have a psychic disorder."

The Christian counseling which my friend started was aimed at showing the woman the way out of her psychic distress. First he asked the patient: "Did you subject yourself to sins of magic?" The question was answered by a confession. The attempt to show her the way out of occult subjection from the Bible ended in the patient beginning to tremble and swear and curse terribly. On the other hand she gave the impression that she was longing for help and deliverance. Since at every prayer typical twitching motions appeared, the counselor got the impression that he could be dealing with demonic influences or even possession. This opinion was augmented through the observation that the patient grew quiet every time he commanded in the Name of Jesus. One day after commanding the dark powers she could even believe in the redemption of Christ and in the forgiveness of her sins.

After this promising beginning the counseling turned into a dramatic battle. The first phase of the battle was a knife attack. After the patient had learned to believe in Christ the preceding day, she had a relapse on the second day and attacked her brother-in-law with a knife. After he had commanded the powers of darkness in the Name of Jesus, the well-known battle pause followed. The attacker quieted down and even apologized for her behaviour. The same day the patient attended an evangelistic meeting led by her counselor, and in the end she partook of Holy Communion. As she was about to receive the bread at the altar she began to tremble. The brother-in-law observed this and inwardly commanded the powers. She then could take the bread quietly. While receiving the cup the same thing happened. Again the attentive counselor commanded inwardly with the same result. The patient was strengthened by this and went home with joy.

The second phase of the battle led to a psychic short-circuit. After an eight day visit at her brother-in-law's home, the patient again had to return to her family. Each time she returned to her relatives her condition got worse. At that time Billy Graham held a meeting in Zurich. My friend sent the woman an invitation and promised to call for her in his car. The patient accompanied him to the stadium. During the sermon she trembled all over. The brother-in-law prayed with her. Afterwards she was quiet again. A few days later she had another relapse. She had tried to commit suicide and had been taken to the hospital. The doctors thought the patient was living in a wrong environment. The counselor had a different idea. In the meantime he had studied the terrible occultly infected family history of this woman. There was no dark magic art which had not been practiced by this family. He found a great similarity to the case history of a woman, Gottliebin Dittus, over which Pastor Blumhardt had wrestled for 18 months. In the hospital the patient could not sleep in spite of the strongest sedatives. After her release she was turned over to a psychiatrist. He ordered her to be committed to a mental hospital. She was treated with insulin shocks and prolonged sleep but there was not the least improvement. Out of my many years of experience with such patients it must be said that they do not belong into he hands of the psychiatrists but of the expert Christian counselor. Mental illnesses and many groups of emotional illnesses belong to the sphere of psychiatry. Demonically subjected people do not belong into the hands of the doctor but of the Christian counselor. But as a matter of fact there is an extreme lack of expert counselors who are in a position to handle such subjected people.

The third phase of the battle brought the usual routine excitements and then again periods of quiet. The counselor's church held a week of evangelistic services. The sister-in-law was invited for this week. The patient heard one message, ran out angrily and shouted: "I am going to take my life. I'll make an end." Her brother-in-law intercepted her and took her into his study. The patient was still angry and shouted: "Something is going to happen tonight. Either I or the evangelist who gave the message will die." Her brother-in-law answered: "Nobody is going to die. Jesus is victor." He prayed with her. She finally folded her hands and prayed too. She walked quietly out of the room and had a restful night.

The fourth phase of the battle introduced a new factor into the case. The next day, a Sunday, the patient took part in all three services without special invitation. In the evening she made an appointment with the evangelist. The stranger heard her confession and like Brother V. her counselor, he had the impression that demonic powers were at work. He asked the confessing woman: "Did you ever engage in sorcery, magic, spiritism, fortune-telling or similar things?" This question was answered in the affirmative. Then the evangelist commanded these powers to withdraw in the Name of Jesus. In the meantime Brother V. had received more information about the occult activities of the patient's mother. Therefore, after the counseling session of the other evangelist, he prayed: "Lord Jesus, deliver my sister-in-law also from the sins and subjections of her mother." At this moment the patient had a violent outburst of temper. She attacked the counselor. Suddenly a strange voice spoke out of her the following words: "This is my daughter. She must die." Brother V. immediately recognized the situation. He replied at once: "No, she must not die. You as her mother have to give her up." Then the strange voice answered: "My daughter belongs to the devil. I have subscribed her with blood to the devil as a child." Brother V. commanded this voice: "You spirit of the mother have no more rights here. Jesus' blood is enough for your daughter. She is redeemed through Christ." Then the strange voice replied: "If I give up my daughter, I'll lose my mind. I'll be insane if I give in." — During the time of this battle, the patient's mother was still living. — Brother V. answered: "Even if you'll lose your mind you must go for good and give up your daughter." After this strange conversation the patient was completely exhausted. But she could pray quietly. In this phase of the battle, a strange being had made itself known out of the patient. It was a similar situation as in the Biblical report in Mark 5. Such things can be found in the Bible, in church history, in the history of missions and in the present time. I have written down a number of such cases.

The fifth phase of the battle revealed a new fact, which threw more light on the story. The next day the visiting evangelist challenged his audience to a decision for Christ. The patient decided in her heart: "I want to be one of those who follow Christ." For a few days she was full of joy. After the third day she had another relapse. At the breakfast table she suddenly stopped eating. She began to tremble. Her face was distorted into a terrible grimace. In her fear she called for her brother-in-law. He rushed to her side and prayed with her. This time she did not quiet down during the prayer. She declared that there must be another strange power within her. She would often see a strange figure without recognizing who it was. Brother V. then commanded the unclean spirit to depart from her. Then a voice began to speak out of the patient but it was a different voice than before. This second voice explained: "I won't leave her. I have been inside of her for a long time already." Brother V. asked: "But who are you?" The voice said: "I am an old gypsy." At this moment the patient grabbed the bread knife on the table and tried to attack her brother-in-law. Brother V. grasped her arm and prayed. The patient quieted down, put the knife away and began to cry. She was completely concious the whole time.

The sixth phase of battle brought the climax of this dramatic fight. The next day the second voice again began to speak out of the patient. The voice was mocking. "You are all scared. You are trembling." Brother V. answered: "No, I am not afraid." Then ugly laughter came out of the patient again. "You can't do anything. We are legions and defend ourselves to the last. The doctors in the mental hospital did not know either who was behind the sickness." For the first time the wife of the counselor interrupted and called: "Then drive into the swine, if you are legions." "No, we want to stay in people. We'll drive into you." Brother V. answered: "That is impossible. We belong to Christ." "Then we will drive into your wife." "You can't do that, she also belongs to Christ." "Then we will drive into your children. We have already made your son sick." As a matter of fact the son Theo had been sick. "We would have made him worse if we would have had permission." Brother V. replied: "You are not allowed to do that. All of my children belong to Jesus." "Then we'll drive into the church and destroy it. We know which souls aren't on guard." "You can't do that either. Christ is guarding his church." At this moment the patient started to run away. Brother V. held her and pushed her down on a couch. She jumped up and tried to get the knife again. Then Brother V. commanded the legions to come out of her. While commanding suddenly many voices moaned out of the patient: "Won't you finally stop praying?" Brother V.: "No, we will not stop till all of you have come out." The voices asked: "What do you get by one single soul?" Brother V.: "To the Savior one single soul is worth more than the whole world." The voices: "We will not come out of the woman, or else she will go home and be a witness to her surroundings and take away souls from us. Stop your praying now. Some one else is also praying in the house." Brother V. did not know that his children had gathered in a room and were praying also. Therefore he answered: "Yes, the Savior is also praying for you." The voices in agitation: "No, no, He is not praying for us." At this moment the patient cast a hateful look at a picture of Christ. Brother V. replied: "Yes, he does not pray for you spirits, but for you, poor human being. You may become free through Christ." The voices: "We can't stand your praying much longer." It was a three hour long battle between Brother V. supported by his wife and ten children who were praying in another room and these powers of darkness. After this long struggle the counselor once more commanded the unclean spirits to depart. Suddenly the patient became quiet. She cried and started to pray. After her deliverance the patient suffered from terrible physical pains for one day. On the last day of the evangelistic services she gave a testimony for

Christ. The pain disappeared. On Sunday she joyfully took part in Holy Communion. While earlier she always had had the feeling as if the powers of darkness were trying to choke her while taking part in Holy Communion, she could now do so without disturbance or hindrance. Christ had won the victory in the battle over this poor, bound human being. For this purpose the Son of God was manifested that he might destroy the works of the devil.

Otto Vogt.

## 9. THE STRONGER ONE

Near Madang in North-East New Guinea is the mission hospital Jagaum. One day a young Papua Christian Koimbo was brought to the hospital, who had been the first one to carry the Gospel from the coast to his tribe in the mountains. The tribe to which Koimbo belonged were idol worshipers and only a few of his tribesmen were brought to believe in the Name of Christ and to renounce the spirits. This small group of course was bitterly persecuted by their fellow tribesmen. Often Koimbo was in danger of his life. But his enemies did not dare to kill him openly and devour him as it had been the custom until ten years ago. So they besought a notorious magician to get rid of him. He was immediately ready for it because he also feared for his influence. So he took the offered payment and began his devilish work. He called to the spirits to punish Koimbo because he as a Christian was interfering with their power.

Koimbo used to meet with the few Christians in the jungle for it was impossible to hold a service in one of the village huts. The villagers would have prevented that. But also in their meetings in the jungle the Christians were not unobserved. So once again Koimbo held a service. At the same time the magician practiced his sinister art — then the terrible thing happened. Koimbo had just read the Scripture in a loud voice when suddenly he stopped, held his head and called: "I can't see anything." His friends jumped up and led him out into the open. They waited for him to regain his sight but it was in vain. Koimbo remained blind to the heathen's delight.

After a few weeks spent in his hut, inwardly and outwardly weakened, his friends brought him to the hospital at Jagaum. When they led him out of the village, all villagers stood before their huts making fun of him and deriding him and the old magician triumphed: "Now you see, our spirits are certainly greater than the Christian's God."

In the hospital Koimbo was received very warmly. But after a thorough examination the doctor could confirm only that both of his eyes had been completely blinded and that there was no prospect of him ever regaining his sight. This was a difficult message for the sick man. He was close to despair.

In the evening the white nurse walked through the ward and stood at the bed of Koimbo. "How are you?" she asked him. He felt for her hand and said: "O sister, that I am blind is not the worst thing to me. But that I can't feel God's hand any longer and must believe that I am delivered to the evil spirits, that is the most terrible thing." This word pierced the nurse's heart. Should it really be like that? Should the demonic powers keep the victory? It must not be so.

"Koimbo, we want to pray to our Lord. He will certainly hear us. The evil spirits mustn't have the last word. Jesus is victor." So the two of them began to pray to the Lord Who had once opened the eyes of the blind and had delivered the daughter of the Cannanite woman from the power of the demons. The whole night they reminded the Lord of His promises till the day dawned.

Then suddenly Koimbo shouted loudly: "Sister, I can see you. I can see you. Anuto (God) has helped me. Anuto is great." All nurses and assistants came running. All were deeply moved and full of joy and gratitude.

Now Koimbo felt the urge to return again to his village. He wanted to be a living witness unto his fellow villagers that Jesus is the stronger one who crushes the powers of hell.

## 10. IF THE SON THEREFORE SHALL
## MAKE YOU FREE ...

One day in our mission station in Lishui a messenger arrived with the request that a few Christian women should come to the house of the salt dealer at the water gate. The salt dealer and his wife were members of our church. I started out accompanied by a few faithful Christian women, the Bible woman, the wife of the evangelist, the wife of the mission teacher and the wife of the apothecary. In the house of the dealer we found a terribly emaciated form of a woman. She was introduced to us as the sister-in-law, who had been carried in a portable chair over a six hour way to get help from the Christians' God.

At first we received the usual illness report. The relative had been afflicted by Fan yiao, the demon who causes so much trouble among the heathen. Help had been already sought from many idols. Everything had been in vain. Now the God of the Christians should prove his power on her. At this report the wife of the salt dealer became frightened, for Fan yiao is a terrible plague. None among the heathen is safe from it. The Christians also are uneasy about it. But she could not turn her sister away and prevent her from staying in her house.

After the close of the report my companions and I first started to sing the song: "The great physician now is near." Our Christians love this song because the Name of Jesus is often mentioned. They say: "The devil flees when he hears the Name of Jesus." Then the Gospel of Jesus was told to the possessed woman. At first she did not understand much of it. She only grasped one thing that Jesus could help her. To this she clung with all of her power. We prayed with her. I rejoiced to see the strong child-like faith of my Chinese companions. The plagued heathen woman was also taught to call on the Lord Jesus for help and to trust in Him. — The next day we returned again. With great joy we heard that the night had passed without disturbance. We now made arrangements among the Christian women that each day two others should visit the heathen woman and pray with her. We saw that this plagued woman could sleep peacefully night after night without any disturbance.

One day during the visit of the Christian women the heathen woman was quite desperate. She cried: "He found me again, he found me again." During the night she had been plagued again. She explained the demon had come to her in the form of a black cat and had molested her. Immediately our Bible woman asked: "Did you have anything to do with the idols again?" At first the heathen woman did not want to come out with the truth. Finally she was ready for a confession. Her husband had visited her and was very happy about the healing. When he left he said to his wife: "You know that we have promised a fat pig to the idol if he heals you. Now

I will go and keep this pledge. After all one can't be sure who helped you." The woman agreed. The husband left with this intention. The same night the woman had again been victimized by the enemy. Our Christian women advised her to send a messenger immediately to her husband that under no conditions should he sacrifice anything to the idols. The honor belonged to the Lord Jesus alone who had touched and healed his wife. This advice was followed immediately.

After this bad experience the terribly frightened woman begged to be taken to the mission station. But we did not have room for her. Then the Bible woman said: "I will take her in. She can live in my room with me and sleep in my bed." Four people often sleep together in the large beds of the Chinese. The heathen woman then moved in with the Christian woman. She stayed there for three weeks and heard the Word of God daily. Because she remained well all the time she wanted to return home in November. At her departure she said: "If I remain well then I will come for Christmas and celebrate with you." At the beginning of the holidays we waited for her return. When she did not come on the first day of Christmas our faithful Bible woman declared she would set out on the long journey to see the healed heathen woman. But it did not come to this. On the second Christmas day our heathen woman arrived radiantly and brought a large thank offering with her. She had remained free in all of the past weeks. Because of a great flood she could not travel on the first day of Christmas. Our worry had been unfounded. The delivered woman was full of praise and gratitude for the help of the Lord. Her belief in Christ had been strengthened through this experience. She was the only Christian in a completely heathen area. For years during our visits we could see that she remained faithful to the Lord Jesus. Later we lost contact with her because we could no longer travel into this area because of unrest caused by bands of robbers and the Russian-Japanese war.

## 11. IN MY NAME SHALL THEY CAST OUT DEVILS

On one of our outstations we had a faithful Chinese evangelist, who had much authority in prayer. In the area of this mission station there were comparatively many cases of possession. It is astonishing with what understanding and accuracy the Chinese can differentiate between mental illnesses and cases of possession. In this they are superior to many European psychiatrists who only know cases of serious hysteria but not of possession. If this evangelist had the impression that he had met with a case of possession he called together his prayer group. Sometimes they prayed and fasted for some days till the Lord gave help and deliverance to the bound one. Once the faithful prayer warriors had prayed and fasted for 52 evenings for a possessed woman who lived next door to the Gospel meeting hall till a complete victory was given and the woman was delivered. A special example shall be reported which shows the difficult battle for the souls of men.

Close to the mission station a family was living where through the generations one member was always possessed by Fan yiao. If the possessed one had been destroyed, Fan yiao passed over into another member of the family. The family had never ceased to fear because of this trouble. When I was on this mission station the father had just perished under terrible agonies. Now the demon had taken hold of an old aunt. It was to be expected that the old woman would not last long. The mother and daughter were the only ones left of the family. With fear they looked forward to the day when Fan yiao would take possession of them. As my co-worker and I brought the Gospel to this area both of the women came under the Word of God. With joy they received the message and learned to trust in Jesus. But it did not come to a complete commitment of their lives to Christ. During this time the old aunt died. The daughter was at the funeral that was held by the idol priest. During the mourning ceremonies the girl was hit by misfortune. Fan yiao had taken possession of her. Immediately the frightened mother brought her to the Jesus hall and asked the Christians for help. The prayer group met for the young girl. On the first evening the plagued one became free.

After some time the girl married a young heathen man. She had to take this step because according to Chinese custom she had been already betrothed for many years. After the wedding the heathen parents-in-law forbade the young woman to attend the Christian meetings. They took away and burned her Bible and song book. From this time on Fan yiao again had power over her. Strange voices spoke out of her and she was unable to do any work. This condition frightened her in-laws. They asked the evangelist to come and pray with their daughter-in-law. The evangelist started on the way with his prayer group. The heathen family promised to let the young woman follow her faith. They also wanted to get her a new Bible and song book. The prayer group withdrew for prayer. The same evening the young woman was free again. Depression, fear and despair left her. She could get up and work immediately. She was overjoyed about the fast help.

Then Sunday came. The young Christian wanted to start on her way to the service, but the heathen parents-in-law were sorry about their promises. Again they burned the Bible and song book and did not let the woman go to the service. On the same day Fan yiao again was ruler. Again the young woman was so plagued at night that she was not able to do any work during the day. The heathen recognized now that this Jesus Christ was not to be trifled with. They had experienced the constant change how the demons would immediately take over if she were to withdraw from Christ. In their fear they had their daughter-in-law taken to the Jesus hall in a carrying chair. Again the proven prayer group came together for the young woman. Already three evenings had been spent in prayer and fasting. This time Fan yiao did not yield. The evangelist felt that now the time had come to act. He approached the possessed woman in the Name of Jesus commanding the unclean spirits to depart from her. In Chinese he used the strongest language: "Your time is over. Now you must leave in the Name of Jesus." Suddenly a man's voice called out of the young woman: "Who can stand this praying? This is unbearable." From this moment on the woman was free. Now her parents-in-law agreed that she could follow her faith. She was not bothered any more. Fan yiao never returned.

In these last two reports from the Chinese mission field several things become clear. There are not only sicknesses of the mind, the soul and the emotions, but there are also demonic influences and possessions. The symptoms of possession have the same characteristics in China as in Europe and in other parts of the world. Their characteristics also agree with the symptoms of possession in the New Testament. Possession is a condition which passing all time and national boundaries always has the same peculiar character. Because this concerns a

Biblical fact the psychiatrist who is not a believing Christian will not be able to understand it. Who can only think in three dimensions will never understand the sphere of the divine and the demonic. Over the phenomenon of possession stands as a radiant reality the victory of Jesus over all dark powers. He who has given himself over to Jesus partakes of His power. Jesus Himself says (Mark 16, 17): "In My Name shall they cast out devils."

## 12. THE VICTORY OF CHRIST

A missionary worked among a magically infected tribe on New Guinea. Many magicians held their fellow tribesmen under their ban. The Christian mission made only little progress. In her prayer the missionary often felt approached by a terrible power. She asked all her friends at home for faithful intercessory prayer that the dark ban in her area should finally be broken. She did not only feel a terrific spiritual battle in her area but she also experienced strange threats by wild animals. Every time when she wanted to visit a certain village in which a well known magician carried on his evil work, snakes met her on the way so that she was forced to turn back. She looked upon these animal experiences as accidental until one day she found out that it was no accident. During a missionary trip she came into this mentioned village on her return journey. Unsuspectingly she entered one of the unknown huts to bring the Gospel message to the occupants. While she spoke to the woman she felt a terrible power overwhelming her. She had the impression as if she would be killed from behind. She turned around and observed that the man who sat in the corner looked at her with a fixed stare. She was startled and felt banned by this look and knew at that moment that the dark power emanated from this man. She tried to pray inwardly but due to this threatening look she could not do so. Finally she knew no other way out but to command in the Name of Jesus. Now something extraordinarily strange happened. The staring man collapsed and laid whimpering and moaning on the floor. He crept towards the missionary. When she left the hut he still crept after her whimpering and moaning. This experience reminds us of the story of the Philistine god Dagon (1 Sam. 5, 3) who laid before the Arc of the Covenant in the morning. Afterwards the missionary found out that without her knowledge she had been in the hut of the chief magician. The natives also knew about this man's ability to make wild animals yield to him.

## 13. THERE IS POWER IN THE BLOOD

I wanted to conduct a week of evangelistic services in a small village. I stood well-prepared, I thought, in front of a group of people who had gathered in the school house. But I had more and more difficulty in speaking, for I felt as if somebody was holding my mouth shut. I walked home covered with perspiration. One thing was clear to me: I had met here with a resistance, which I, as a young evangelist, had never before experienced. Could I use my prepared messages here at all? Did not these people need something completely different? With such thoughts occupying my mind I climbed into my bed in an attic room and turned off the light.

There, what was that? It stood before me like a big, dark shadow and I could hear a voice which said quite clearly to me: "If you dare to continue this evangelization I'll kill you, for these souls belong to me." What was I supposed to say? For me there was only one answer: "If the Lord commissions me, then nobody can stand in my way." But again I heard the sinister voice saying: "All right, I'll kill you then." At this moment I was seized by cramps in my arms and legs which spread all over my body and finally concentrated on my heart. I was unable to move and turned cold. I laid there for two hours till the cramps subsided again. I did no longer doubt that the enemy wanted to kill me. But at the same time I also knew that he could never do it unless the Lord would permit it.

The days which followed were very difficult for me. Soon I found out where the strong resistance in the village came from. In many houses the people practiced fortune-telling and magic. Some were plagued by the powers of darkness under whose ban they had fallen. I wanted to prepare new messages for the evangelization, but I was unable to do it. I wanted to pray, but I could only kneel and sigh. Night after night I was seized by the same cramps as on the first evening. They happened always at the same time but without the apparition. I was in great distress and did not know what to do. I had the strong conviction that the Lord had called me, otherwise I would have given up this evangelization.

I turned to some brothers for advice but they did not take the matter seriously. Finally I was led to a dear, elderly servant of God who was experienced in these things. I could talk to him. I could confess to him that I, as a minister called of the Lord, did not dare to lay hands on people who requested it in order for them to be delivered from their ban. Was I only called to be a preacher? Must I be helpless when they turned to me for counseling in their greatest need?

The Lord Himself had led me to this elderly servant of God. He helped me decisively. What I received from him, I should have been taught in seminary. But perhaps I would not have understood it then. But now, standing in the midst of the battle, the guidance of the elderly brother was a great help to me. Was it something new that he told me about the power of the blood? No, I knew this power and yet it all seemed so new and great to me. Not only did the cramps stop after I consciously put myself under the protection of the blood of my Savior, but I could also see this power at work in the lives of others to whom I could now give counseling help. Power and victory were given to us through the blood of Jesus.

"For this purpose the Son of God was manifested, that he might destroy the works of the devil" (1 John 3, 8).

Otto Haeni, Evangelist, Switzerland.

## 14. DEPRIVED OF POWER

This experience happened on a spring day of the year 1959. A dentist called us on the telephone and inquired about the kind of work we were doing. He wanted to know the aim and purpose of our telephone counseling ministry and how we handled it. We gave him the requested information. Then he declared that he would visit our office personally. We made an appointment. The dentist appeared at the appointed time and showed signs of extreme nervousness. He could not sit quietly on a chair for an instance and we noticed how he stared at us fixedly. We felt that a sinister atmosphere emanated from him and that somehow he tried to put us under his spell. The counseling is usually done by two of us.

Because both of us had the same strange feeling, we retired for a moment in order to pray. Afterwards an animated conversation developed. When half an hour later he left us we actually felt his sinister influence on us. Fervently we prayed for cleansing through the blood of Jesus Christ that we would not fall prey to this evil power.

The next morning the sinister stranger called again and asked whether we had felt anything last night. "What were we supposed to have felt?" we asked in return whereupon he hung up without a word. On the second morning the same thing was repeated. Again he hung up and once more we discussed the puzzling behaviour of this man.

A few days passed. Then he requested us to pray for him. Then he called us again. He told us that the devil had given him specific instructions to fight our telephone ministry. In great distress he told us that while he had been a student in Marseille and Paris he had subscribed himself with his blood to the devil. Now he could not return as much as he wanted to follow our advice. A few days later he called again. He confessed in great desperation that he had tried to kill us and had used his proven method for it. But it had failed. What he had tried to do to us had fallen back on himself repeatedly. A much stronger force and power went out from us than the one he possessed. He explained further that he could not stand it any longer. He could not accept the Word of God, because he belonged to Satan to whom he had subscribed himself and who was now driving him to his death.

The next day we received a post-card. A cross was inscribed in the upper right-hand corner and underneath were the words of the sinister stranger: "When you receive this card, I will be dead." Soon afterwards the local police called us. They reported that the dentist had shot himself. They had found his body in his room, next to his Latin recipe book, the so-called Mirror of Solomon. If we would be interested in it, they would turn it over to us.

Over many years the unfortunate man had plagued the people. He had not been a good dentist, but in spite of it he had had a good practice. But because of his contract with the devil he had been driven to destruction by faith in God. Does not this experience show in all clearness that the power of God, the power of Jesus Christ, is incomparably greater and stronger than the devil's power? And does it not also show that the prayer of the saints is not in vain? Jesus has conquered hell and devil, He ist the stronger one. He has deprived the darkness of its power. "And having spoiled principalities and powers, he made a shew of them openly, triumphing over them in it" (Col. 2, 15).

Werner Ambuehl, Evangelist, Switzerland.

## 15. THE NAME OF JESUS

It was shortly after the Second World War. Fortunately I had escaped out of Russian hands. Then I began to suffer from depressions caused by malnutrition. Hunger and exhaustion had done their destructive work on me. My emotional disturbances continually increased. I turned to neurologists for help. One doctor prescribed opium drops to quiet me down. But another doctor took away all medicines. He took me to his sanatorium and tried psychotherapy. Both treatments had little success. Opium had made me worse and psychotherapy was only successful as long as I was with the doctor.

I tried to reenter my former profession as a Protestant minister. With the increasing work load my sickness also increased. Those were very dark days. My wife called a doctor again for consultation. One day when I was at the lowest ebb the Lord intervened. A preacher visited us, but I immediately went out of his way. In my condition I did not want to talk to anybody.

The evangelist talked to my wife. He told her that he had the impression that he should pray for me and lay hands on me according to James 5, 14. At first I determinedly rejected it. The Biblical laying on of hands was completely unknown to me in practice even though I was a minister. In seminary I had hardly ever heard anything about these Biblical customs. Therefore I did not agree with the desire of the preacher.

But my wife won. She talked to me from the Bible about the laying on of hands. I gave in. The brother prayed with me under laying on of hands. Nothing happened. The next day he came again. When he heard about the fruitlessness of his efforts, he inquired about subjections in my life. I got hot inside. What subjections was I, as a Protestant minister supposed to have?

The brother told me about the many magic charmers who lived in the area where I was born and the many sins of witchcraft. He also told me that sins that my ancestors had committed in this regard could still subject me. Slowly it dawned on me. My father had been sick in his youth. Medical help had been in vain. Therefore his mother had taken him to a magic charmer. The magic treatment had been an immediate success.

The evangelist now pointed to the First Commandment. It says there: "Visiting the iniquity of the fathers upon the children, unto the third and fourth generation of them that hate me" (Exo. 34, 7). Now he asked me whether I recognized the magic healing of my father to be a sin of witchcraft. I admitted it. We went down on our knees. In spite of my minister's title this was also strange to me. I repented over the sin of my ancestors and over my own sin. It was a repentance to life. In faith I could receive the forgiveness of my sin and committed my life to the Lord Jesus.

As he had done in the preceding days, the evangelist again laid his hands on me and prayed with me. Suddenly all depressions left me. I was filled with an unspeakable peace and lightness. I had never before experienced this feeling. I was almost floating, I had become so light. This overflowing joy remained for weeks and months.

For the first time I unterstood the word in Phil. 3, 20: "For our conversation is in heaven". I felt like my feet did not touch the ground at all. Everything, my life, my days which had been so grey were transfigured by the love of Christ. The whole Bible, also my ministry looked completely different to me.

When after some time I went to see the doctor again, he examined me and came up with the following finding: amazing progress in both physical and nervous areas. The depressions never returned. This miracle happened to me after I had been a minister for several years. And it was a humble preacher who had been Jesus' messenger to me.

What had happened to me by the grace of God was felt also in my church. My congregation sat up and listened to my new kind of preaching. My main emphasis was now to lift up the Name of Jesus before all the people. The Word did not return void. People were converted. In the surrounding areas, where I was called to minister now, there were also small revivals from time to time. It had been impossible before to hold weekday services and prayer meetings, but now they sprang up into being without any special effort. He Who had started the fire was continuing to tend it.

The Name of Jesus had become the great strength of my ministry. This Name meant power to me, the power of salvation unto many. It has become my burning desire to tell all who listen to my message, what the Name of Jesus holds. "Neither is there salvation in any other: for there is none other name under heaven given among men, whereby we must be saved" (Acts 4, 12).

Rev. Berthold Schoof, Germany.

# Other books by the Autor

Seelsorge und Okkultismus
Der Spiritismus
Wahrsagen und die Folgen
Die Magie
Der Aberglaube
Belastung und Befreiung
Die Nachfolge Jesu
Liebe — so oder so
Feuerzeichen
Der Höhenflug
Jesus lebt
Jesus siegt
Jesus heilt
Jesus unter uns
Jesus heute
Jesus im Alltag
Mit Jesus unterwegs
Unter der Führung Jesu
Vom Sieg Jesu

EVANGELIZATION PUBLISHERS
Berghausen Bd. (Germany)